# THE STAR PEOPLE
# SERIES

*Revealing Today's New Truth*

**THE STAR PEOPLE** tells how thousands of men and women are discovering that they are descendants of visitors from the stars...

**REVELATION: THE DIVINE FIRE** shows how the "gifts" of prophecy and divination are manifestations of humankind's developing "star consciousness..."

**GODS OF AQUARIUS** examines today's wave of UFO sightings and reveals their link to encounters with Higher Intelligences...

**REFLECTIONS FROM AN ANGEL'S EYE** actually tells us how to take the next evolutionary step...into the New Age...

And now **THE SEED**—Brad Steiger's most personal book ever, revealing his own childhood encou[...] trial!

D1569857

*THE STAR PEOPLE Series\**
*by Brad and Francie Steiger*

THE STAR PEOPLE
REVELATION: THE DIVINE FIRE
GODS OF AQUARIUS
REFLECTIONS FROM AN ANGEL'S EYE
THE SEED

*\* All available from Berkley Books*

# BRAD STEIGER
# THE SEED

A QUICKSILVER BOOK

BERKLEY BOOKS, NEW YORK

THE SEED

A Berkley Book/published by arrangement with
Quicksilver Books, Inc.

PRINTING HISTORY
Berkley edition/March 1983

ISBN: 0-425-05845-X

# Chapter One

## MY QUEST BEGINS

The New Age is here now. It is a spirit within us, a vision, a seed, a presence that is beyond Time and able to enter us now if we will permit it.

*David Spangler*

I always felt that man is a stranger on this planet, a total stranger. I always played with the fancy: maybe a contagion from outer space is the seed of man. Hence our preoccupation with heaven, with the sky, with the stars, the gods, somewhere out there in outer space. It is a kind of homing impulse. We are drawn to where we come from.

*Eric Hoffer*

When I was a child, I witnessed a most extraordinary occurrence. It was on an October night in 1940. I was not quite five years old, but I could already print my name in spiral notebooks and on paper shopping bags.

I remember clearly that I had been sitting on the edge of my bed, looking up at a harvest moon, when I heard the sound of someone walking outside on the crisp autumn leaves. Since

1

my parents, my three-month-old sister, and I lived on an Iowa farm two miles east of town, the footsteps of anyone approaching the house—especially after dark—was an occasion of some importance.

I was struck at once by the fact that our collie dog, Bill, was not barking at the intruder. Normally, either friend or stranger would be met by his loud and persistent yelps of welcome or warning.

When I heard a tin washtub being dragged from the pump at the well, curiosity and a small sense of alarm prompted me to get off my bed and to walk closer to the window to investigate. I was astonished, rather than frightened, by the sight of a smallish man settling the tub beneath our kitchen window. The peculiar little fellow was dressed in a one-piece coverall, something like the kind that Dad wore when he worked on machinery; but the stranger's outfit was very tight, almost molded to his body.

Bill was crouched by the side of the house, but he was not moving or making a sound. It was as if he were as transfixed as I by the unexpected visitor.

The kitchen curtains were open, and the light from the kerosene lamp illuminated the little man's head and upper body as he raised himself on tiptoes to peer in at my mother and father. I could see his very large, round skull, two pointed ears, and long, slender fingers as they grasped the window sill.

I didn't really see his eyes until he must have sensed that he, the watcher, was being watched, and he turned to look at me from a distance of no more than seven feet. Although we were physically separated by a windowpane, the transparent barrier did nothing to refract the tingle of shock and surprise that I received from those enormous, slanted eyes with their vertical, reptilian pupils.

I drew in a sharp gasp of air, and my heart began to thud at my chest. I had just begun to think that I had caught a brownie or an elf unaware, but when I saw that the little man had no hair, barely any nose, only a slit with a sardonic curve at either end for a mouth, I felt a small buzz of fear. And those eyes were so emotionless and detached.

But the more I looked into the shadowed depths of those eyes, the calmer that I became. They were already disproportionately large for such a small head, but now they were expanding even more. They seemed to grow larger and larger, more and more enchanting, until the next thing I knew it was morning.

The tin washtub was still against the kitchen wall, but Bill had left the house to see about his morning duties overseeing the pigs and the cattle. It appeared as though our nocturnal visitor had left the big collie completely untroubled.

I could not absorb the visitation with anything approaching his canine casualness. I ran into the kitchen to shatter all possibility of Mom and Dad having a quiet breakfast. I had exciting news to tell them: A little man of highly unusual appearance had spied on them while they had sat talking at the table.

With great good humor they dismissed my report as a colorful example of childish whimsey, but I did receive a more complete hearing than many children of my generation might have been granted. I was, after all, descended from the famous Danish storyteller Hans Christian Andersen. My mother, too, had always had a vivid gift for creating imaginative tales of make-believe, and she had had a number of mystical and eerie experiences in her youth.

Dad's more rigid evangelical Lutheranism caused him to be more cautious concerning spiritual dimensions beyond those prescribed from the pulpit of St. Olaf's, but he was always quietly tolerant of the beliefs of others. He advised me, though, that it would be much better if I went right to sleep at bedtime and did not sit on the edge of my bed and permit my imagination to wander.

Mom smiled, winked at Dad, and said that I was certain to follow in the tradition of our illustrious ancestor. She knew that one day I would be writing stories in books for boys and girls to read, just like Hans had done. In the meantime, she agreed, I must not sit up nights and frighten myself.

But a potent seed had been activated within my psyche. No amount of adult persuasion could alter the evidence of my personal experience. We were not alone in the universe. There were other intelligences walking about who resembled us, who seemed curious about us, and who might even care about us in some way.

Magic was real. I felt it every time that I stood under the kitchen window where the little man had pulled the washtub.

It was damp in that sheltered corner, and moss and toadstools grew next to the stone of the foundation. It was a magic place. I could feel it.

I became convinced that there were creatures of enchantment all around me. I had seen one, after all. No doubt there were others who slept in the shadow of lilac bushes by day, who gamboled at night, and who would grant me marvelous powers if I could but convince them of my sincerity.

I found another magic place in the woods that surrounded our farmhouse. It was a circle of brownish soil that seemed to

Based on Steiger's description of the humanoid that visited his family's Iowa farm when he was five years old, artist de Paschal has drawn a likeness that recaptures the author's close encounter.

resist the lush green grass that sprouted everywhere else on the moist floor of the grove and apple orchard.

Whenever I stood in the circle, I could sense the presence of the little man; I could hear music, strange and hauntingly beautiful; and I glimpsed the form of a beautiful fairy princess who had enormously large, fawnlike eyes.

Over the next few years, Grandma Dena, who lived in the big house in town with hundreds and hundreds of books, helped me to piece together a kind of historical overview of the intelligences that I would one day come to call simply the "Others."

It seemed as if these Others were humanlike in appearance, but they often expressed themselves during their visitations by producing miraculous healings, insightful illuminations, and spiritual revelations. Such wonders, issuing as they did from beings who transported themselves in fiery or mysterious globes of light, had inspired human witnesses to call them angels, saints, fairies—or, on occasion, devils or mischievous elves.

I had not been given any spiritual revelation that I could recall, but I had been given proof of their existence. I had seen one of the Others.

Although my faith in the reality of the visitation remained unshaken, when I went to school I soon learned that teachers, however kind and patient in other areas of childish idiosyncrasies, were likely to administer heaping doses of ridicule upon little boys who claimed to have observed smallish men with snake-like eyes. And recess periods brought the reality therapy of organized teasing and mockery from my classmates. I understood at once that I must become far more selective in my choice of confidants.

My Sunday School teachers—all of whom were hardworking, pious farmwives—proved to be even less receptive to my magical experiences than the instructors at the public school.

There was no such thing as Magic, I was repeatedly told. Miracles and gifts of the Holy Spirit had occurred during the days of Jesus, the disciples, and, later, the apostles; but if such things happened today, they were more than likely the work of Satan masquerading as an Angel of Light.

There was no Magic. There was only planting and harvest, death and taxes, war and peace, marriage and children—and trying to get through life with as much dignity and as little strife as possible. Heaven would be the reward for those who recognized the way things were. Hell would be the punishment for those who transgressed the immutable laws of God and Nature.

Books helped me to keep Magic alive. Books helped to nurture the seed that a strange visitor had planted in my psyche on an October night.

Then, on August 23, 1947, when I was a boy of 11, I died—or, for a time, seemed to die—as the result of a terrible farm accident.

My body lay crushed and bleeding, sprawled where the mangling, metallic blades had dropped it. The Real Me had moved several feet above the tragic scene, only dimly aware of my association with the dying farmboy. I had become my essence, an orange-colored spheroid, intent only on soaring toward a brilliant light higher above me.

I felt blissfully euphoric, and I glorified in a marvelous sense of Oneness with All That Is. As I related in my book *The World Beyond Death*, from time to time, whenever I would feel a fleeting pinch of sorrow over leaving my family and friends

I would be shown *something* that I can now best remember as a kind of great tapestry of life, which demonstrated in a very dramatic way the order and the rightness of existence. The glimpse of this cosmic panorama must be classified as an ineffable experience, impossible to translate into physical expression; for whenever I try to explain it, whenever a memory of it is stimulated, my brain blanks during an attempt of its full description.

I was in and out of my body during a desperate 140-mile run to reach a hospital in Des Moines where our family doctor thought my life might be saved. Whenever the Real Me would enter the body of the dying eleven-year-old boy, it seemed to reject the choice and return to the dimension of reality where there was no pain.

I am aware of no entity or echoing voice assuring me that I must return to the physical clothing of flesh, but I did at last return to the body with such force that I sat up, shouted, and pushed an intern off-balance just as they were about to begin the surgery. It took the calming tones of love and caring from a Roman Catholic sister to pacify me until the anesthesia could take deeper effect.

During the two weeks of my hospital stay, the sisters seemed to have sensed that I had been "somewhere" and had seen "something" and they would ask me again and again about my experience as a spirit-essence, traveling between the two worlds.

A mystery had been pierced, they told me. I would never again have to ask the troubling question about whether humankind survived the experience of physical death. I would be able to testify that there was truly an existence which transcended the material realm.

I have never felt "chosen" or "special" because of the visitation or the near-death experience, but I have regarded myself as having been blessed with two experiences before the age of puberty that permitted me to know what so many others must accept by faith alone.

I am of the opinion that every thinking man and woman asks himself or herself Three Big Questions:

1. Why was I born?
2. Will I survive physical death?
3. Is humankind alone in the universe?

Because of that multidimensional or otherworldly visitation when I was five, I understood that humankind is not alone. We share this turf with other entities, both physical and nonphysical.

Because of what could have been a fatal accident, I understood that we do survive physical death in our spiritual essence.

And because of the two experiences mentioned above, I perceived the meaning of my life: I am to testify to the truth that the human spirit is eternal and that we are not alone in the cosmic scheme of things. My mission is to tell others of these eternal verities, to be what my adoptive Seneca Indian name, *Hat-yas-swass*, represents: "He who testifies."

Rather early on in my adolescence, I began more and more to perceive life as a quest. I came to believe that humankind is meant to strive toward a meaningful goal through a series of progressive, experimental episodes, each of which will contain a number of hidden messages which must be deciphered and understood before we may proceed on to the next sequence of life experiences.

To me, my quest was a spiritual one above all—regardless

of the physical and material challenges which would be presented to me along the peaks and valleys of human experience.

I agreed with Professor Mircea Eliade, who saw that the contemporary world was constantly moving toward secularization, but who doubted that the "total man" could ever be completely desacralized.

"Secularization is highly successful at the level of conscious life," Eliade wrote in the preface to his book, *The Quest*:

> Old theological ideas, dogmas, beliefs, rituals, institutions, etc. are progressively expunged of meaning. But no living normal man can be reduced to his conscious, rational activity, for modern man still dreams, falls in love, listens to music, goes to the theater, views films, reads books—in short lives not only in a historical and natural world, but also in an existential, private world and in an imaginary Universe.

Although I had been contributing to local newspapers since I was fifteen, it was in 1956, when I was a twenty-year-old student editing an award-winning college newspaper, that I became a professional writer with sales of my short stories and articles to national magazines. At the same time, I attempted to sell pieces on the paranormal and on metaphysics, but there were few takers. The fifties were not receptive to consciousness expanding.

In 1957, shortly after I turned twenty-one, I began to teach high school. I was still selling short stories and articles to a wide variety of periodicals, but a full load of teaching chores, two extracurricular activities, and a seemingly endless number of after-game dances to chaperone left me little time to maintain the kind of productive writing schedule that I desired.

I resolved, though, that I would prepare "tons" of material that would be ready for the Cosmic Printing Presses when the moment on the Celestial Clock struck "Awareness Time." For the next three years I read extensively, wrote industriously for my personal files, interviewed Spiritualist mediums, and sought to perfect my individual methods of meditation and creativity.

It was sometime in 1959 that I first put down the rudiments of a personal creed that, several years later, together with my soulmate and coauthor Francie's added inspiration, would become our Starbirth Creed. It was during late night hours with the works of Emerson and Thoreau and their New England Transcendentalism; Dostoevski, Kierkegaard, and Sartre and their Existentialism; William James, Ivar Lissner, Marcus Bach and their visionary experiences, that my mission expressed itself in a statement of belief:

I believe the birth of all religions lies in the mystical experience of the individual and that all theologies and dogmas are but secondary growths superimposed.

I believe there is a Supreme Being, Timeless and Universal, to whom all men and women may reach out and receive strength.

I believe humankind is part of a larger community of intelligences, a complex hierarchy of powers and principalities, a potentially rich kingdom of interrelated species—both physical and nonphysical. Among these intelligences external to humankind are multidimensional beings who care about our spiritual evolution.

I believe humankind's one truly essential factor is its spirituality. The artificial concepts to which humankind has given the designation of sciences are no truer than dreams, visions, and inspirations. The quest for absolute proof or objective truth may always be meaningless and unattainable when it seeks to define and to limit man's Soul.

I believe the Soul is eternal, evolving higher in spiritual vibrations, seeking to return to the Source from whence it came. I accept the Karmic Laws of balance and compensation and the concept that the Soul lives many lifetimes in order to gain learning experiences for its good and gaining.

I believe technology plays a far smaller role in the lives of nations than the spirit, for the essence of man is his intellect and his Soul. Machines, associations, political parties, and trade balances are but transitory realities, which must ultimately wither, decay, and come to nothing. The only lasting truths are Soul, imagination, and inspiration.

I believe that each man and woman, in moments of quiet meditation, may learn to enter the silence, enrich the Soul, and achieve a spiritual linkup with the blessed Harmony that governs the Universe.

* * *

By the time that I moved on to college teaching in 1963, I had begun to sell short stories at a rather brisk pace to the mystery and fantasy magazines. Mercifully, my writer's ego was receiving enough of the blessed balm of encouragement to keep at the typewriter.

Then, too, my files on the paranormal, the strange, the mysterious, the unknown were bulging to the bursting point. And I had managed to sell an article on reincarnation, another on ghostly mysteries of the sea, an eerie one on haunted houses, and a couple of others on bizarre occurrences. I probably averaged about fifty dollars a piece for the articles on the mysterious, but I was beginning to crack the materialistic shell that the publishing world had erected around itself.

While I was teaching world literature and creative writing in college, I edited a literary review and published widely in the mystery, fantasy, and general interest magazines. I was also a correspondent and a stringer for numerous trade papers and journals.

By the time that my first book, *Ghosts, Ghouls and Other Peculiar People* was released in 1965, I had published over one hundred and fifty short stories and nearly four hundred articles in such publications as *Alfred Hitchcock's*, *The Saint*, *Fantastic*, *Saga*, *Exploring the Unknown*, *Family Weekly*, *Parade*, and a great variety of other magazines.

As an instructor at a Lutheran college in the Midwest, I had to be relatively discreet with any discussions of metaphysics in the classroom, but I had begun to lecture upon the paranormal and ESP and I had found high interest among my audiences.

A lot of my colleagues in the speculative fiction genre had sport with my speaking to psychic, UFO, and metaphysical groups. But, as I stated earlier, I had always wanted to believe in Magic and in the reality of my serpent-eyed, elflike visitor. Parapsychology, metaphysics, a study of the paranormal, regardless of their rather bizarre and often embarrassing side trips, were all ways by which modern man was keeping Magic alive. And just maybe, somewhere along the cosmological trek, some serious-minded man or woman would find the bridge that linked the separate realities and would make the translation from the weird to the real.

Just after the First World War, Bronislaw Malinowski observed that the Trobriand Islanders in the South Seas resorted to magic whenever they were confronted by situations in which they felt threatened by danger or uncertainty, whenever they were faced by circumstances in which they did not feel in control. Well, God knows that in our technologically hyped super society, we often feel every bit as threatened by forces beyond our control as did those simple islanders. Are there any among us—other than the professional fatalists—who have not tried his or her absolute damndest to manipulate the new gods of the machine and the old gods of the earth? Who has not prayed to a deity, practiced a private ritual, or carried a personal charm?

In the December 1980 issue of *Psychology Today*, George Gmelch and Richard Felson presented their study of magic on today's campuses, "Can a Lucky Charm Get You Through Organic Chemistry?" Of the 450 students Gmelch, an anthropologist, and Felson, a sociologist, tested, about 70 percent used magic in such situations as gambling, danger, examinations, sports events, face-to-face encounters, and in illness. The young men and women used productive magic (a good luck charm), protective magic (crossing one's fingers), personal rituals, and lucky numbers.

A study of the kinds of students who practiced magic revealed that 90 percent of them claimed a belief in modern science, and about 80 percent of them also expressed a belief in God. While it was true that students who used magic were likely to believe in ESP and the supernatural, the strong believers in science were just as likely to use magic.

"Generally," Gmelch and Felson learned, "the use of magic accompanied more practical, scientifically approved, actions. Exam magic, for instance, did not replace studying hard, but supplemented it."

Magic, the researchers learned, reduced anxiety. Seventy percent of the students interviewed said that using magic made them feel better. And the more that people care about the outcome of an activity, the more they will seek to use magic to attempt to guarantee a favorable end result.

"This leads to an interesting anomaly," Gmelch and Felson wrote. "As societies become more technologically advanced, people become more highly educated, and as a result, presumably less inclined to use magic. However, emphasis on achievement and success also increases with modernization. Since people seem to use more magic when they care most about the outcome of a performance, the use of magic in some activities may *increase* with modernization, not decrease."

Interestingly, though, most of the students interviewed gave intellectual lip service to the assertion that, even though they practiced magic, they didn't really believe in it very strongly. They seemed to be aware that the practice of magic did more to reduce their anxiety than it did to bring about favorable results.

"The psychoanalyst might say that belief in magic probably persists beneath the level of awareness," Gmelch and Felson wrote. "We prefer to say that students are not just playing it safe when they practice magic. They are not sure it works, but they are not sure it doesn't either. . . ."

In January of 1966, I went to New York City to complete the final rewrite on my book, *Valentino*, which director Ken Russell would one day convert into the cinematic vehicle that would serve as balletmaster Rudolf Nureyev's motion picture debut. Although I had managed to secure a contract on a book about poltergeistic phenomena, *Strange Guests*, prior to the publication of the movie sheik's biography, my reputation was as a writer of short stories in the mystery and fantasy genres. (*Ghosts, Ghouls and Other Peculiar People* had been published by a very small house in Chicago, and had been largely unread.)

Therefore, no one was really aware of my "bizarre interests" when, at an editorial luncheon, my editor on *Valentino* began to speak, rather self-consciously, of the ghost of a man who had committed suicide in his apartment, prior to his occupancy. It seemed, he confessed, that the ghost of this man had manifested itself before him on several occasions.

My agent spoke up and said that I had long made a "hobby" of investigating such phenomena. Before I could speak to the matter of my editor's ghost, another person on the editorial staff spoke up and asked if I could interpret a troublesome dream that had been perplexing her. I was pleased that so many sophisticated New Yorkers seemed truly interested in my opinions about such "far-out" matters, and I sallied forth with great gusto.

That was the beginning of my nearly ninety books in the metaphysical and paranormal fields. Shortly after I had returned to the college classrooms, I had a contract for a book on UFOs, *Strangers from the Skies*, and another on strange occurrences, *World of the Weird*.

Editors at Ace, Award, Dell, Belmont, and other houses were receptive to my establishing entire series of books on things that went bump in the night. Soon I was writing volumes on reincarnation, ESP, ghosts, Atlantis, and more UFOs. And to supplement my files, I was traveling across the United States and Canada interviewing witnesses to poltergeistic, extraterrestrial, and multidimensional phenomena.

Not all editorial personnel were respectful toward my work, however. Although they were decent as human beings, some considered my efforts as "kook" books.

I realized that I would have to set about educating the publishing world, as well as the general audience, about the validity of metaphysics in their daily lives.

It occurred to me then that the books on which I must concentrate at that moment in Space and Time would have to be relatively sparse on theorization and spirituality. The majority of editors wanted me to supply them with books that would consist of short, punchy chapters—the briefer the better. They wanted the person on the subway, the airplane, the bus to be able to read one more quickie chapter before he reached his destination.

I rationalized that there were still more people on the primary level of metaphysics than there were on the graduate level. I would, for the time being, provide the books that would be their "A-B-Cs" to higher consciousness.

I pulled open my file drawers and my notepads and started mining the material that had been awaiting its moment before an audience. Carefully I arranged them in a well-wrought, progressive order. Short chapters can be effective if they lead to a unified theory.

Actually, everything went quite well. A couple of years ago, David Techter, who served for so long as *Fate* magazine's excellent book editor, remarked in his column that the "health" of the psychic-metaphysical field was due in large part to my steady paperback propagandizing during the years 1966–1972.

Such praise, in my opinion, provided me with at least partial justification for having forged ahead with my series of original paperbacks, for having gritted my teeth and withheld my theories until the time was right, for having swallowed my pride when so many of my books received a sensational and garish packaging.

Ever since my college days, I have tried my best to abide

by the ancient Greek admonition that a sound mind lives best in a sound body—which is, in a sense, another way of working Magick upon the mental and physical aspects of Self.

I have never enjoyed team sports, because there are always a couple of guys who simply cannot leave things at the play level. There are always those to whom winning at sports is the single most important thing in the universe. Winning becomes so integral to their manhood and their continued existence as sovereign entities that they feel justified in humiliating their teammates, insulting their opposition, and arguing, shouting, punching at both.

Sports are supposed to be our funtime, our recreation, our constructive way of exercising the body and letting off a little steam from our boiling nerves. I cannot see their purpose as creating animosities, rivalries, and additional frustrations and pent-up emotions.

Shortly after I graduated from college I discovered body building and weight lifting, and they seemed at once harmonious with my essential lone-wolf personality. *One*: Working out with weights did not require either teammates or an opposing squad. *Two*: A workout could be conducted at any time, night or day, without putting out a summons to gather other participants. *Three*: There would never have to be anyone yelling at me to lift faster or slower. What I did and how I did it was up to me.

Several years after I had established both weights and writing as essential elements in my life pattern, I discovered that the repetition of hoisting the barbell and the monotony of elevating the dumbbells had become meditation in motion. I found that I could put my body on automatic pilot, so to speak, and while the arms were pumping the barbell, my creative self would be soaring free through Time and Space to focus on solving the sticking point in my writing. To my complete delight, I found that weights and writing were complementary on a level which I had never suspected when I began pumping iron.

Working with the weights had also another bonus for me. Having been reared on Iowa farm work, there was a stubborn residue of frontier mentality that would sometimes rear its bucolic head and accuse me that there was something unmanly about earning a living as a writer. Men should put bread on the table by getting calluses on their hands and dirt under their fingernails. There was something sissified and suspect about the Ichabod Cranes of the world—those men who bought their livelihoods with their brains instead of their brawn.

True, I had my ancestral link with Hans Christian Andersen to remove some of the pressure, but my father was known for his physical strength; Uncle Irwin was a giant; Mom's brothers were all tall, tough men. And the local histories described my great-grandfather Christopher as "...a man of great strength and character, who soon turned the wild prairies into fertile and productive fields. He became a leading spirit in the community, church, and schools, and helped build up many enterprises."

Such atavistic accusations had troubled me considerably when I attended college each fall. While I was sitting in a comfortable library researching a report for political science, I was uneasily aware that at that very moment, bundled up against nearly freezing temperatures, men were getting in the harvest of field corn.

After graduation, when I was at my writing desk struggling over the proper adjective for a sentence in a short story, I was torn by the knowledge that, while I sat in front of my air conditioner and my typewriter, there were men who were working in the blistering sun to put up hay for their livestock.

The "iron pills" once again cured me of a debilitating mental disease—that of creating self-tormenting and energy-distracting thoughts of guilt over the fact that I earned my living by "unmanly means." Who could call me a sissy when I was two-arm curling 200 pounds and bench-pressing 400?

In order to balance my insecurities, my career struggles, and the probable reality that I would be a schoolteacher and an Ichabod Crane forever, I had bulked up to the point where it was impossible to buy any other than custom-tailored clothing. At six feet tall, I weighed 210 pounds, had a forty-eight-inch chest, eighteen-inch biceps, twenty-eight-inch thighs, and a thirty-five inch waist. I looked like a bouncer, rather than an author. Hemingway would have been proud of me, but editors weren't buying writers by the pound.

My bulk and my bulges began to decrease in direct proportion to the sale of my books and their acceptance by a growing multitude of faithful readers. Now at age forty-six, I find it a matter of mental and physical balance to exercise both my body and my brain each day.

I have abandoned the drive for Herculean proportions, but I still derive a wonderful easing of tensions and a clearing of the cluttered head when I religiously pump iron. The current regimen, however, requires lower weights and higher repetitions, so that I am building for endurance, not for enormity.

I have melted my body weight down to 185 pounds, and I haven't put a tape measure to my chest for eight years. I know with full assurance that I want to be remembered for my metaphysics, not my muscles; for my brains, not my biceps.

# Chapter Two

## LEARNING TO PLAY THE REALITY GAME

> Science is based on one kind of experience—that of perception and discursive symbolism of language, including mathematics. But there are others also, different in basic experiences and mode of expression. Such are the universes of art, human values, mystic experience, and religion . . . which in some respects appear more profound and nearer reality.
>
> *Ludwig von Bertalanffy*

Throughout the course of my quest, I have come to believe that the "Others" who interact with us are in the process of playing a teaching game with the more enlightened of our species. Those members of humankind who choose to enter such a contest will soon notice that their concept of reality is gradually being changed. In the teasing fashion of a Zen riddle or a Sufi joke, we are being provoked into a higher consciousness.

As I wrote in *Mysteries of Time and Space*:

It may be that mankind has been invited to participate in a bizarre kind of contest with some undeclared cosmic

opponents. Man may have been challenged to play the
Reality Game; and if he can once apprehend the true
significance of the preposterous clues, if he can but master the proper moves, he may obtain a clearer picture of
his true role in the cosmic scheme of things. The rules
of the Reality Game may be confusing, extremely flexible, and difficult to define, but play man must—for it
is the only game in the Universe.

From time to time I am chided by those who feel that I am
too careless in suggesting that life is a game. Life, they re-
monstrate, is serious business. One does not "play" at it.

But I believe that when we are able to apprehend the true
significance of the Reality Game, we will thereby attain such
control of our life and our abilities that we will be able to
confront all aspects of existence with the same ease and freedom
with which we would enter a game.

In *Myths To Live By*, Joseph Campbell describes a very
special manner of polite, aristocratic, Japanese speech known
as *asobase kotoba*, "play language." In this convention, one
would *not* say to another, "I see that you have arrived in Tokyo." Rather, one would state, "I see that you are *playing* at
being in Tokyo."

Campbell tells us that the idea behind *asobase kotoba* is that
the person addressed is in such control of his life and his powers
that for him everything is play, a game. He is able to enter
into life as one would enter into a game, freely and with ease.
What *has* to be done is attacked with such a will that in the
performance one is literally in play.

Such is the attitude that Nietzsche termed *Amor fati*, love
of one's fate. It is what the old Roman Seneca referred to in
the oft-quoted saying: "The Fates lead him who will; him who
won't, they drag."

I believe that, throughout the ages, those who chose to enter
the Reality Game had the opportunity to be provoked into higher
spirals of intellectual and spiritual maturity. I am convinced
that we can interact with the Other and be guided toward ever-
expanding mental and spiritual awareness.

If you choose to come with me and play the Reality Game,
I know that we will find ourselves receiving a clearer understanding of our true roles in the Divine Plan. We will find
ourselves directed to a level of awareness where we may more

readily attain a state of Oneness and self-sufficiency.

Through personal experience I have learned Nine Rules which I consider essential to helping me win at the Reality Game. These Rules have also become mottoes and guidelines for me, and I want to share them with you now.

### 1. IN THE BEGINNING WAS THE WORD, AND THE WORD WAS "ADJUST."

One must stay open to changes, however dramatic in his or her life, and be prepared to adjust lifestyles to accommodate the new status of What Is.

One must develop his or her inner resources to the point where changes and encounters are not viewed as catastrophes, but as challenges.

### 2. LIFE IS A SERIES OF INTELLIGENT COMPROMISES.

One need never compromise that element within his or her spirit that is the most complete expression of one's private ethics and morality, but one does need to get along in life.

Remember, we are all in this life together.

We are all children of the same Father-Mother-Creator-Spirit, each of us seeking to survive on the physical plane in the best way that we can, and each of us struggling to achieve higher awareness on the most meaningful spiritual path that is available to us.

It is foolish to argue, to fight, or to die for unimportant issues or for principles that effectively serve only the few who rigidly cherish causes designed to profit materialistic enterprises.

### 3. MOST OF WHAT WE BELIEVE TO BE FACT IS REALLY A MATTER OF TASTE, OPINION, OR PERSPECTIVE.

As Nietzsche once observed, "There are no facts, only interpretations." There are few things on the Earth plane that are really true in the eternal sense of TRUTH.

Nearly all things that we believe to be true are but matters of perspective.

Test this aspect of reality for yourself. Draw up a list of all the most complete and erudite definitions of scientific truth that were held fast as physical laws and realities . . . in the Middle Ages. Do the same for the Renaissance. For the Industrial Revolution. For the turn of this century. For before World War II.

How many of those hard and fast Truths and Facts remain valid and supportable today?

And now try making up a list of spiritual truths! Consider all the causes and crusades for which men and women have fought, died, and been tortured and persecuted.

How many were actually *spiritual* truths?

How many were, in reality, matters of politics, prejudice, greed, and perspective?

Now bring it home to *you*. How many TRUTHS did you hold so firmly that you would have staked your Soul on them when you were six . . . seventeen . . . twenty . . . that you still hold as sacrosanct today?

Rule Three helps you to remain tolerant of others, and it certainly helps to keep you out of senseless arguments that sap energy and emotional strength better expended in more productive areas of your life.

### 4. WHAT YOU AVOID RUSHES AFTER YOU.

This has been stated by others in words to this effect: that which one fears most will most often come to pass.

I believe that this Rule is due to the laws of polarity which exist on this planet. Those laws extend to the point where the more good you do, the more agents and energies of negativity seem attracted to you.

This Rule is another good case for keeping balance in all aspects of one's life. It is always better to stand up to conflicts eye-to-eye than to permit them to stalk you steadily behind your back.

Problems simply will not go away on their own accord. You must learn to dissolve the energy of negativity.

### 5. IT IS ALL RIGHT TO USE AN OCCASIONAL CRUTCH AS LONG AS YOU NEVER MISTAKE IT FOR A THIRD LEG.

By this Rule, I mean that from time to time we all need a little help from a source of strength external to ourselves.

No, I am not referring to a Supreme Energy. I'm not talking about any situation that dramatic.

I am talking about crutches . . . and about being realistic and strong in their use. If you've never been in a situation where you felt for a time as though you simply couldn't cope, then you are in no position to judge.

Sometimes we are just too sensitive, too sympathetic, too sentimental, too loving, too forgiving for our own good; and the world can make fools of us and squeeze in on our hearts and souls until we find ourselves screaming for help. The pain has become too much to bear.

If that has never happened to you, then you are numbered among the most fortunate of humans—or you are a Light Being reading this from a dimension of higher reality. If you had already got all your physical learning and growth experiences out of the way, then you had no reason to incarnate. You would already be a candidate for Total Oneness with the God Self.

Sometime or other you might really feel that you must take tranquilizers, moderate dosages of alcohol, or other chemical crutches to get you through an unbearable time in your life. Take them. But take them realistically.

Say words to the effect: "I must now take———————to help me for a *brief* time. This is as if I have broken my leg, and I need a crutch for a time. When I am through the crisis, I will no longer use———————on a regular basis, just as I would no longer use a crutch after my leg had healed."

By stating such an affirmation, the danger of habitual usage will be lessened.

We never have the right to judge another's pain; but in our individual experiences, we owe it to ourselves never to come to accept a crutch as our third leg. Recognize it for what it is: A device to help you function until you are healed. Then discard it in favor of your own "leg," your own inner resources.

### 6. THE STRIVING IS MORE IMPORTANT THAN THE GOAL.

I am indebted to one of my spiritual mentors, Wolfgang Goethe, for this great realization.

When I was an eighteen-year-old college student studying *Faust*, I was struck with the beautiful truth of one of the underlying themes of this great masterwork of literature: The striving is more important than the goal.

Of course the goal of higher awareness, transcendence, and transformation is vital to our spiritual evolution. But, you see, if you live always in the positive attitude of *striving* toward that goal, regardless of the obstacles in your path, then, in one sense, you have *already* reached your goal.

To believe with all your essence that it is better to give than to receive, to share than to hoard, is largely to have gained your goal of selflessness.

To live as though your life shall be transformed through your positive acts of disciplined Magic is already to have begun your transmutation from the clay of humanity to the cosmic cells of angelic intelligence.

It comes down to a matter of attitude. The attitude of striving toward a goal, of having made a total commitment to a cause, has a greater effect upon one's lifestyle, upon one's treatment of Earth's fellow creatures, upon one's ability to withstand the crises and despair of living than will the final accomplishment of the mission.

Who is responsible for having built the Great Pyramid? The ones who placed the first block in place, or the ones who fitted the capstone on its peak?

The placing of the capstone was, of course, the goal of the architect, for it signaled the completion of a mighty task of timeless significance. But without the setting of the first block and the striving of thousands of others, the capstone would have been a reminder of failure, not a monument of victory.

The achievement of your transformation as an evolved entity signals the accomplishment of many of your Soul's physical lifetimes as expressed in your present life experience. But it will be your attitude of commitment toward such a goal, your striving to attain such a capstone of life, that will make you a person *worthy* of transcendence.

One's goal, then, is simply the last step in a long journey— a niche that would have no true meaning or importance without the first step having been taken and the attitude of commitment that made possible all the steps in between.

### 7. WORK WITH YOUR EGO.

The Ego—and I'll define him as a conscious, concerned Self—is really a marvelous fellow. He helps us tie our shoe-laces, walk across the street without being struck by traffic, and fork our food into our mouths instead of our ears.

You know how he can get inflated and demand attention beyond his importance, but I want to dismiss that problem by stating that you should learn to develop self-esteem and positive assertiveness rather than egotism. Ego-*ism* is self-acceptance. Ego-*tism* is tedious, insufferable, and will prevent anyone from wanting to take a long bus trip with you.

The problem of Ego that I wish to discuss with you is the one that prevents you from entering a deep state of meditation.

It is in those deep states of altered consciousness that your Feminine-Creative Self can really speak to you and aid you in becoming a successful player in the Reality Game. It is standard practice in our psychological jargon to call this area the Un-conscious, but that always seems like such a nothing name and such a contradiction in terms. I think it best to understand that there are several levels of consciousness and that our doorway to creativity and spiritual illumination comes from deeper—"higher" if you prefer—levels of our inner selves.

Your Ego has been paying close attention to all the indoc-trination that you have received since earliest childhood, and since his basic job is your survival, he is reluctant to permit you to enter altered states that will remove you from his juris-diction and his ceaseless monitoring. The Western World has never really encouraged the mystical experience; and, remem-ber, your Ego is the product of several hundred years of Western culture.

This tireless pragmatism is unfortunate, for quite likely all people are potential mystics, just as all people are potential poets, artists, and musicians. We have all daydreamed, entered trancelike states, ecstasy, and so forth; so we all are aware that there are many levels of expanded consciousness.

Yet the orthodox recognize only two states of conscious-ness—sane and insane. And your vigilant Ego does not want anyone to think that *you* are insane! He'll snap you back to wakefulness any way that he can whenever you start to drift into an altered state.

Treat your Ego with honesty and with love. Come to terms with your Ego right now. Arrive at a clear understanding of how you wish to structure your spiritual development program.

When you are entering an altered state, your Ego will often intrude to harp at you about a bill that needs to be paid, a responsibility that needs attention, the tip of your nose that needs scratching.

You will accomplish nothing if you mentally shout at your Ego and tell it to go away, to leave you alone. It may shrink off for a moment or two, but it will come back with its insistent demands even stronger than before.

Understand its position. Look at your Ego as if it were your older, loving brother.

Imagine a situation wherein your brother comes into the room and reminds you of an important responsibility. Annoyed by the interruption, you turn and shout at him to leave you alone and to be quiet.

Hurt, shocked, your brother would leave. But then, after a few moments of consideration of your rudeness, he would probably burst angrily back into the room and demand to be heard.

So it is with your Ego, who exists only to serve you and to help you survive the slings and arrows of outrageous life on the Earth plane. Never tell your Ego to shut up and leave you alone when you are practicing any meditation or spiritual exercise.

Instead, say gently, "I recognize the importance of your message. I will listen to you and pay close attention to what you say as soon as I have completed my meditation. Thank you for caring. Now, please leave me for a while. I will return to you after a time."

Speak firmly, but with loving recognition of the Ego's energy. Don't be afraid to develop secret multiple-personalities.

You really must learn to speak to your Ego and your Essential Self as the special friends that they really are. Don't be the least bit self-conscious about this. The more creatively that you can speak to your Selves, the more you can structure Reality.

**8. WHAT IS REAL IS NOT NECESSARILY WHAT IS REALITY.**

To become an effective player in the Reality Game, you must become as a child. Truly, you must become childlike (that's not *childish*). You must look fresh at reality. You must not be afraid to apprehend the world around you on intuitive and subjective levels.

Those children who were fortunate enough to have parents who indulged them in fantasy play become adults who are capable of deep trance states, deep religious experiences, empathy, compassion, and the ability to respect different world views. They are also the adults who are the most flexible in dealing with people.

What is real?

I often cringe when I hear people say that a profound teaching message received in a dream was *not* real. Just a dream, they shrug.

Just a dream, indeed! Dreams have changed the course of individual lives and the course of nations.

I, like so many others, have been receiving dream teachings since I was a child. I have utilized those nocturnal instructions to write books, plan lectures, structure my life.

Everything that humankind has ever created has begun with a dream, an image in the mind, an inspiration. Physically, none of those things are *real*. Yet humankind makes nothing *real*, that is, physical, that did not first have its seed in the mind.

If it were not for dreams, visions, and inspirations, humankind would still be cowering in caves, begging fire from a lightning storm, seeking succor from the nameless dread of darkness.

Those dreams, visions, and inspirations which I have received on my quest are among the truly *real* blessings that I have experienced. And I have loved the challenge of transmuting their magnificent energy into fully productive material-plane manifestations of books, articles, seminar programs, and cassettes.

You have often heard it said in metaphysical circles that you can create your own reality. More correctly, that which you create is your basic *attitude* toward reality and how you choose to deal with it in every aspect of existence. You can, indeed, practice fantasy play and enter the Reality Game fully armed with a positive approach to dealing with any type of hardship that you may encounter.

One of the most important accomplishments of the man or woman on a spiritual quest is the learning of effective fantasy play in order to enable him or her to face all of life's crises in a confident and a creative manner.

The first step in such an approach to life is to learn that every event may be dealt with from several perspectives. The particular perspective which you select as your construct, must not only be *believed* in by you, *you must become it*.

When Jesus spoke of *being the way*, he was expressing the great metaphysical truth that one must transcend identification with a path or an attitude. He was instructing all those on a spiritual quest to *become totally One* with their "way."

Jesus also spoke of his "way" as working best in shared relationships with people who agree on a perspective of reality and who can, thereby, provide important mutual feedback to reinforce that perspective.

Jesus spoke of "two or more" gathering together to ask for certain things, to agree on the means of achieving them, to become detached from ordinary reality, to reinforce one another's commitment to replace the conventional with a new construct, to agree to submit to the reality of that new construct, to agree to serve the new construct of reality.

Certainly, two or three harmonious energies will always be better than one; and when you have a group of other spiritual seekers with whom you join in a consensus of reality, you may accomplish *anything*. You will literally be able to refashion, reshape, and reconstruct reality to be harmonious with your world view.

*There are times, when, like everyone of mortal clay, I sit in the still small hours before dawn and feel nostalgia for the things that might have been.*

*Often I study the photographs of my children, Bryan, Steven, Kari, and Julie and reflect upon sadly transient moments of happiness in a past that sometimes seemed to have belonged more to another than to myself. I look at the pictures of a birthday party, a Christmas-gift opening, a childish chin with a Band-Aid, and I marvel at the ability of shutter speed and lens opening to trap a memory on film emulsion and contact paper.*

*There are the pictures from Disneyland in October of 1969.
I will always remember Julie's excitement when we turned a
corner of the idealistic Disneyland Mainstreet and came face-
to-face with Mickey Mouse and Goofy. The young people inside
the huge, misshapen cartoon heads and the hot, uncomfortable
baggy clothes were good enough to pose for me and to endure
my insecurity with a camera until I snapped six pictures "to
be sure."*

*Although Bryan is now nearly twenty-five, he will be forever
twelve years old in the photographs. Kari is almost twenty-
one, and Steven is twenty-two, but they will eternally stand
there next to Goofy as an eight-year-old girl and a ten-year-
old boy. And Julie, seventeen now, stands there at the age of
three, just a little doll of a girl, looking up at Mickey as if he
were an animal-headed deity blessing mortals with a fleeting
presence.*

*In those moments of an acute awareness of times past, I am
sometimes powerless to control the stinging sensation in my
nose and eyes that brings the tears running over my cheeks. I
am helpless in the face of the realization that nothing on this
Earth lasts forever.*

*How, in those hours, do I wish that I had the ability to write
a book in which we all might have lived happily ever after.
The children would have understood that I wasn't angry at
them when I yelled at them for playing the stereo too loud,
that I wasn't uninterested when I didn't attend all of the ball
games and band concerts and PTA meetings, that I wasn't
unsympathetic when I didn't always listen for very long when
they had problems in school or with their friends—it was just
that I always had deadlines that had to be met.*

*If only I had had the power to write a book in which we
might have lived, I would have created a life-script that would
have been so idyllic, so tranquil, so positive, so wonderful . . .*

*And I would want them to understand just why the divorce
happened. How the real problem was that their mother and I
had married when we were just kids. There had been a time
when we had known each other, cared for one another, and
supported one another emotionally; but we had grown up in
different corners of the house and with different headsets from
the ones in which we had entered the marital union. Most of
all, my belief construct had become an embarrassment to her.*

*It is during such moments of attempting to placate myself about the past that I recall my Rule Number Nine.*

### 9. DO THE BEST YOU CAN.

I spent so many anxiety-ridden years of my life attempting to be perfect.

In 1966, a Jesuit priest, who wished to share certain concepts with me, reflected that, from certain of my responses, I must be familiar with Thomas a Kempis' *In Imitation of Christ*. I granted that he was correct, and added that it had been at my nightstand for years, as a kind of bible.

The problem was, in my striving to be as a literal, physical, Christlike person, in my desire to be all things to all men and women, in my wish to be everyone's brother, I not only was losing my own identity, I was experiencing an extensive repertoire of fears and exhausting a catalog of neuroses.

I had to admit at last that it was an impossible task to fulfill each and every person's expectations of who I was to be. Each student has his or her idea of the Perfect Teacher. Each child has his or her concept of the Perfect Father. Each member of the audience has his image of the Perfect Lecturer. And so it went with my sincere attempts to be a Perfect Husband, Perfect Author, Perfect Guru, Perfect Consumer.

Before I became Perfect Mental Patient, I had to come to grips with my dilemma.

I told myself that I tried always to express myself as a person of goodwill. I have never deliberately been cruel, nor would I ever consciously desire to hurt anyone.

I was reared in the Puritan work ethic, and I am programmed to be as productive as my mental and physical energies permit me to be.

Early in life I made a total commitment to raising awareness and to affecting the mass consciousness in a positive way with the testimony of my mission.

Therefore, since I know in my heart that I am doing the best that I can within the limitations that life in the Earth plane imposes upon me, people will just have to deal as best they can with me if I do not fit their expectations of me.

I will endeavor to move through life with kindness, consideration, and as much grace and style as I can. But if I do not dress, speak, look, act, or behave precisely as someone else thinks I should, then, in the words of the philosophical comedian Steve Martin, "Well, excuuuuuse me!"

Do as I do: Rather than beginning each day with a recitation of the emotional terrors, the stressful horrors, the guilt-ridden obligations that lie before you, look at yourself in the mirror, wink, and say, "Hey, Kid, you're all right. Your're doing the best you can!"

# Chapter Three

## *EXPLORING PAST LIVES*

The light of eternity is reflected in the bottom of the soul, like moonlight which shines undisturbed in the depth of a well.

*Kitaro Nishida*

What does it mean to be human?

The psalmist assessed that question and decided that to be human was to be a little lower than the angels.

Shakespeare marveled at what a piece of work humanity was: "How noble in reason! How infinite in facultys! In form and moving, how express and admirable! In action, how like an angel! In apprehension, how like a god!"

I believe that humankind most certainly has the choice to be more than an arrangement of biochemical compounds. We can elect to become the sons and daughters of the Divine, rather than the cousin of the laboratory guinea pig.

I maintain that humankind need not be trapped in the same cycle that imprisons the atoms of hydrogen and oxygen.

And I believe that the exploration of past lives offers us yet another clue to enable us to answer in a more final and ultimate way the troublesome question: "What does it mean to be human?"

The great French philosopher Pascal once gave expression to another aspect of humanity, a side that I have very often seen in my personal consultations. Pascal declared humankind to be a chimera: "What a confused chaos! What a subject of contradiction! A professed judge of all things, and yet a feeble worm of the earth! The great depository and guardian of truth, and yet a mere huddle of uncertainty! The glory and the scandal of the universe!"

In the twenty years that I have been working with past lives' regressions, I have concluded that the great majority of the men and women who came to see me had literally created their own demons in the forms of phobias and fears that they had permitted to consume their energies and their spirits. They seemed to have made conscious choices to be a part of the "scandal" rather than the "glory" of the universe. These same men and women had developed attitudes of despair and desperation, and they seemed willing to fall into Hells that they had fashioned out of their individual realities.

In our work together, Francie and I have come to see that the great value of exploring one's past lives is to provide the individual with an opportunity to acquire practical tools by which he or she might solve current life problems and begin to build a more positive future. Through contact with spiritual guides, we encourage our consultees to choose to examine past life experiences which they need to know about for their good and their gaining. We seek always to promote self-esteem and a true knowledge of Soul purpose, rather than Ego.

On occasion, of course, we do have a consultee come to us with preconceived notions of having lived an illustrious life as a priestess or as an Indian chief; but by asking what that individual truly needed to see for his or her good or gaining, a more fruitful exploration is often made of a lifetime of wretched poverty, an ignoble life of crime, or a sparse existence as a very undistinguished lump of mortal clay. The important thing, of course, is the lesson to be acquired—and the relationship of that lesson to a family member or a friend with whom the consultee is now in contact.

In our past lives' research with those men and women who fit into the pattern profile of the Starseed or the Star Helper, we have found that so many of them appear to remember past lives in ancient Egypt—specifically at a time when they recall an actual physical interaction between humanity and the Star

Gods. Some of our consultees, while in altered states of consciousness, have spoken of having lived in Sumer and of having received instruction from Star Beings.

Briefly, for those who might be coming on all this afresh, the hypothesis advanced in our book *The Star People* (Berkley Books, 1980) is that among our species are people whose genes carry the characteristics of extraterrestrial, as well as human, ancestors. We have named these men and women the "Starseeds." In addition, there are highly evolutionized Earthlings who have accelerated their progression toward the Source and who are to work hand in hand with the "seeds" to assist humankind through a rapidly approaching time of societal and planetary transformation. These people we have named the "Star Helpers." Collectively, both the "seeds" and the "helpers" are Star People, the teachers and the seers who will serve as the midwives during the birth throes of the New World and the New Human.

A good number of the Star People also claim past lives in ancient Israel, and they have mentioned an association with certain prophets of that region.

An astonishing number of the Starseeds appear to remember prior life experiences as victims of the Inquisition, and many of them are cautious about public declarations of their mission because of Karmic ties to that former "time of the burning."

Almost as many Star People—and in many cases, the very same men and women who suffered the Inquisition—report past life memories during the French Revolution and in other great historical struggles against social injustices.

Many of the Starseeds remember past life associations with manifesting, multidimensional guides and teachers; and a good number of them are convinced that the same guide or teacher continues to manifest in their present life experiences.

Certain of both the seeds and the helpers have recalled past life memories of having lived as a prophet, a seer, a teacher, or an inspired holy man or woman, who sought to alert humankind that we are more things than we can imagine. They have told us that Star Consciousness has, in their past lives, enabled them to tap a marvelous, universal energy that allowed them to achieve self-mastery and to work miracles.

Fae, a leader of metaphysical development classes in Alamagordo, New Mexico, has seen herself as a healer in Atlantis, using "gems of light" to accomplish her cures.

"Several times I have had flashes of being in Egypt," she informed us. "I served in the temple, and I was a healer in that life, also."

Brie, an awakened Star Person from Springfield, Missouri, recalls a life-experience as "Dionne, an Atlantean priestess":

> She [Dionne] lived in the women's temple and was the high priestess at the time of the destruction of the temple (not the same as the destruction of Atlantis). She sent out envoys to [what is now] Ireland, Spain, and South America to search for a place to escape the coming holocaust and to establish a women's temple. These missions were too late and did not succeed. The temple in Atlantis was destroyed by irresponsible use (or political sabotage) of the great crystal [a legendary energy source of the lost continent].

James, an administrative systems analyst, from Arlington, Massachusetts, states that in spite of an orthodox religious training from earliest childhood, he seemed always to sense that the philosophy of one-birth was inaccurate:

> It was as if during such periods of instruction that a third presence was felt. At such times the statement, "He knows not of what he speaks," would be silently heard. Rarely would the silent voice be critical; rather, it was said with compassion.
>
> ... Upon reaching adulthood, I had a strong inner desire to reawaken past convictions on the subject. The following are based on dreams, personal efforts, or memory flashes, plus having a vivid recall as a result of contact with a psychic reader. I am extremely careful in readily accepting what is being said. It is only accepted if, intuitively, it feels right or if it sets off additional flashes. ...
>
> *Egypt*: When I first heard the name, "Egypt," I actually felt the warmth of the sun on my skin and the warmish smell of reeds and water ... I knew the waters of the Nile were good, but were also dangerous. Three lifetimes are sensed:
>
> 1. *A military man*, who is a great strategist, but who has no feeling for people, the court, or the priesthood. His only interest is to expand and to promote Egypt.

2. *A peasant or slave* whose frustration with life results in self-destruction.

3. *An old man*, a refugee from another land, who is learned, but has contempt for the primitive culture and its people. I expire alone, extremely bitter.

*Atlan* [Atlantis]: As a child, I resented anyone telling me it was a myth! One lifetime was spent as a high priest in a temple, assisting people to find themselves and to use their lives to good advantage. (What may be a carry-over from that period, or one similar, is my interest in the use of color, both industrially and in the domestic environment.)

My wife, who worked with me, was beloved, spiritually, intellectually, and physically—words were unnecessary between us, as we would both silently "speak" to one another. (Unfortunately, in this lifetime, we have not yet met, although my search continues.) She died as the result of an accident, which caused me, in sorrow, to react adversely. . . .

A few years ago when Francie and I were attending a conference near Los Angeles, we had a very earnest young woman ask if we might provide her with some guidance. She had just learned through a past-life reader that she had been Judas in a prior existence.

"You mean *the* Judas?" I questioned her. "Kissing Jesus on the cheek, receiving the pieces of silver. That Judas?"

She nodded her head sadly. She was, indeed, *that* Judas.

Francie and I glanced at each other, and the unspoken observation passed between us: How many alleged incarnations of Judas, Peter, Mary, Joseph, and yes, Jesus, had we met during the course of our respective researches?

This young lady (we'll call her Cindy) was truly upset—and understandably so. How, she wondered, might she possibly be able to work out so much Karma this time around?

How many lifetimes would it take for her to wash off the taint of a prior existence of the man who betrayed the Master?

Probing gently, we soon learned that she had been feeling very guilty about having "betrayed" a boyfriend for another lover. In fact, she had a pattern rather well established for feeling guilt because of what she would later assess as her weaknesses.

We assured her that she was quite likely not really the actual reincarnation of *that* Judas, but we acknowledged that she might be acting in the vibratory pattern of the Judas Archetype. She had been a "Judas" in the eyes of her former lover, and she had felt the pain of his accusations of betrayal. She had "sold him out," she confessed. She had been bought by another's promises of a better life.

We discussed archetypes with Cindy at some length, and we think we may have convinced her that she was not the present incarnation of the betrayer of Jesus. There is, however, a rather perverse romanticism associated with the character of Judas that may have countered any of our arguments of common metaphysical sense.

During an earlier conference in Arizona we had had occasion to observe the Great Soul Archetypes phenomenon at work in full force.

A number of men and women attending a week-long series of meetings had felt a pleasant rapport instantly upon their meeting. This sensation of companionable warmth soon led to small gatherings at one another's hotel rooms. Group meditations produced some provocative channelings. Higher guidance indicated that certain other men and women who were also attending the conference should be invited to participate in these private meetings.

By the third evening of the seminar, there were fourteen select members in attendance at the special group meditations being held separately from the participants in the organized lectures and workshops. By the fourth evening, it was revealed that the fourteen select meditators were Mary, the twelve disciples, and in the small, pert frame of a young woman, Jesus— all reborn, all reunited wondrously at a conference in Arizona.

During the course of earlier research, I had previously witnessed such holy reunions. While investigating UFO contactee groups, I frequently discovered that it had been revealed to the inner circle that they had lived together before—as Jesus and the twelve disciples. On more than one occasion, they had been just one member short, and they welcomed me with great warmth, as they recognized me to be Philip or James, or whomever, who had been missing.

I really do not believe that we should look greatly askance at such impromptu pageant plays—for that is really all they are on one level of consciousness. Most of the men and women who enact the archetype of a disciple or of Jesus for a few days generally feel somewhat embarrassed about it by the weekend. Later really none the worse for the experience—and sometimes pleasantly more aware—they resume their real lives in the real world with more conviction to fulfill their missions properly than they might have had before the role was offered to them.

Consider the fact that each year at Christmas we have little boys and girls at Sunday Schools throughout the Christian world dress up in bathrobes and halos to carry shepherds' crooks and wisemen's gifts to two of their classmates who are temporarily personifying Mary and Joseph. The baby Jesus is usually a dimestore doll, which, depending upon one's point of view, is no less a sacrilege than having a sincere meditator assume the role for a few days.

It would truly be cause for some concern if the little imitation of Mary should come to believe that she would one day bear the Son of God, just as it would create ripples of potential tragedy if our adult pageant players should assume their auspicious roles on a more permanent basis. When one refuses to relinquish the archetype several days after the houselights have dimmed, so to speak, then professional assistance may be needed for the inflated psyche.

Our culture encourages archetypal enactments far more frequently than the annual Christmas pageants.

As a young girl, struggling to develop an acceptable expression of her psychic sensitivity and her contact with multidimensional beings, Francie was challenged more than once by the question: "Who do you think you are, Joan of Arc?"

How many young poets are nicknamed "Shakespeare" or "Longfellow" years before those seven-year-olds with precocious rhyming ability can identify either of their creative predecessors?

Could any politician, who displayed the slightest autocratic tendencies, expect to escape the accusation of being a "Hitler"?

And already any metaphysician who begins to attract a personal following is questioned closely by skeptics to evaluate his potential of becoming another "Jim Jones" who may set in motion another "Jonestown" of group suicides.

The matter of archetypes in regard to certain kinds of past-life experiences came up recently in a letter from Faye Frost of Broomfield, Colorado. Faye is a freelance writer and a novelist, who has devoted more than twenty-five years to her part-time avocations of hypnotherapist and clairvoyant-psychometrist. In the New Age attitude of sharing research, Faye reported certain aspects of the Star People whom she had encountered over the years:

> My Star People had conscious memories of many of their past lives, and could go into lengthy detail, even without hypnosis. Hypnosis always confirmed their conscious knowledge. Many could trace their soul pattern all the way back to Atlantis. A few could trace the pattern back to other planets.
>
> Several mentioned a memory of being a very young child (around four or five) and sitting someplace where they were alone when a sudden, very peculiar feeling swept over them . . . "I'm only a child! Just look at me— I'm in a child's body! What's the meaning of this?"
>
> They all said that although they were only four or five, they didn't *think* like a child . . . And they always felt so terribly frustrated when their voices and words came out sounding like a small child's.
>
> They remembered being set down on this planet in a spacecraft of some kind and left here, along with a small group of other people . . . They were told it was up to them to pioneer this very lush, green, promising planet . . . and to utilize all the planet's natural resources until their people came back for them. They recalled a feeling of abandonment and fear.

There were other points well taken, including thoughts about the Star People's acknowledgment of Christ Consciousness; then came an aspect of Faye's research that brought me back a bit:

> Many of these Star People have had previous lifetimes as famous authors, actors, musicians, scientists, poets, etc. And all these great past lives have had one thing in common: To contribute some facet of truth to all humankind. (Perhaps that is the reason I found no great military leaders or Wall Street financers among my Star People—although I do not rule such occupations out completely.)

And then she went on to name Star People who allegedly recalled lives as such men and women as Henry Thoreau, Charles Darwin, Albert Einstein, Lillian Russell, St. Teresa of Avila, Isadora Duncan, and Catherine the Great of Russia. What is more, Faye recalled her own past life as Sam Clemens, Mark Twain:

> I recently returned from a trip to Hartford, Connecticut, where I went through the Twain home at 351 Farmington Avenue for the first time in this life....
>
> The look on the tour guide's face (and on the face of the ticket seller) was worth a thousand words. They looked as though they had seen a ghost....
>
> I went back the next morning, and the ticket seller told me as much. She said that for just an instant, she had seen the face of Mark Twain as if superimposed on mine.
>
> But that isn't important. What is important is the fact that I knew every nook and cranny of that house...It was like coming home. Even now, when I look at the color brochure with the photos of each room, I feel the tears starting to flow. I really loved that house as one loves a person...I had never been to Hartford in my life, but I drove directly to the house without the aid of a map and without asking directions....
>
> I have also visited the childhood home in Hannibal, Missouri, and it is exactly accordingly to the recurrent dreams that I had as a young child in this life in Shreveport, Louisiana.

I wrote Faye that I had found her letter most interesting, but I asked her if she might not be willing to theorize that she, as an author, might have begun to identify with Mark Twain at a very early age. After all, I told her, I, too, had, for a time, been so obsessed with Twain that I had nearly convinced myself that I was his present incarnation.

I revealed that I had met at least three other sincere individuals, one of whom was a college professor, who were certain that they had been Mark Twain in their previous lifetimes.

Perhaps, I suggested, there were a number of us who were in the *frequency* of Twain, in the same manner that a physicist might be in the Einstein vibration; a dancer, in the Isadora

Duncan vibration; a churchwoman, in the St. Teresa of Avila vibration; and so on.

In other words, many men and women may be very close to being the same receptive channel for higher energies who are using certain archetypes as models by which to inspire us. And when that Divine transmission is beaming forth its message of guidance, men and women of similar sensitivity may pick up its broadcast—and, at the same time, may also receive impressions of one another.

I think something similar occurs when people approach one another and remark: "You seem so familiar to me; I believe that we must have shared a past-life experience."

The reason that we occasionally seem so familiar to one another need not necessarily be because we have shared a past-life experience. The reason may be instead that we are very close to being the same receptive channel. I might be KI44, and you might be KI45, or KI43; but we are very close to being the same spiritual frequency. Quite naturally, therefore, we might know a great deal about the inner workings of one another, although we have never met physically; and we might certainly know very much about the archetype that has been used to provoke us and to inspire us.

I was pleased when, on March 18, 1982, Faye replied to my query:

> You said, to a degree, what I guess I was trying to say, without realizing it. It is interesting that you yourself have wondered if you were Mark Twain in another life. My question is: Why not? Perhaps all of our concepts regarding reincarnation have been too constricted. Why not five Mark Twains—or a hundred thousand? Using your archetype idea, that would not necessarily make any of them false. (My husband suggested 100,000 Attila the Huns causing havoc today!)
>
> In other words, we would have a *generic* Mark Twain packaged under many different labels, and with many combinations of ingredients. But the generic base would still be Mark Twain.
>
> People I have encountered who, under very deep hypnosis, recall and relive lives as "great personages out of history," all have that sense of *mission*. It would be interesting to find out if all the Mark Twains and Cath-

erine the Greats have pretty much the *same* mission. In other words, a great spirit divides itself into many segments.

Of course, there is always the idea of spirit possession (although I hardly think Sam Clemens was the type for possession, as he was too anxious to get completely off the planet), and of the atmosphere as a psychic storage battery, so that "tuned-in" people are picking up energy patterns still alive and active. Another thought is the idea of the non-existence of time—that past, present, and future all co-exist. Which would mean that Mark Twain is still living his life and doing his thing, and that telepathy, to susceptible people, is the result. (I can't accept that one, though.)

I once met another woman who insisted that she had been Joan of Arc [a past life with which Faye also identifies]. The similarity of our present lives was beyond belief.

Both born in Texas and raised, as only children, by our grandmothers in Shreveport.

Born in the same year, but different birth signs. (She was Cancer; I'm an Aquarian.)

Both our grandmothers were called "Big Mama."

Both mothers worked in the retail clothing business.

Both fathers were interior decorators.

Both of us had married first at the age of nineteen to men of Italian descent.

Both had two boys and one girl.

Both had lived in Buffalo, New York, and Florida.

Both of us had remarried in the same year to men of similar disposition.

Both of us were freelance writers.

And our maiden names were similar, Wood and Ward.

If there's no coincidence, to what extent did a generic Joan of Arc affect us both?

In my own experiments with self-hypnosis, I have guided myself back through what may be other lifetimes which I have shared with Francie. Since I have recorded an induction procedure and the suggestion of a number of general types of emotional scenes for exploration, it is a relatively simple matter to serve as my own regressionist.

Once I reach a deep inner level of consciousness, there is a blur of color before my sense of sight and a swaying, eerie sensation of rapid movement. I seem next to be somehow suspended in a place where there is a swirling, purple mist. I ask my guide to grant me all that I need to see for my good and my gaining, and I am confronted with a flashing montage of symbols which eventually slow down to appropriate scenes of teaching.

I have often received fleeting images of hurtling toward Earth in a vehicle which appears to be in flames. Obviously, I, and several others, survive a crash-landing. Together we view the ruins of what appears to be a vast hominid culture that had been devastated by a series of cataclysms and convulsive Earth changes. We direct our attention toward the inhabitants of primitive villages near the remains of these great cities. It is our intention to assist them to develop spiritually, intellectually, and culturally.

Inadvertently, but unavoidably, this transmission of knowledge and wisdom also creates a longing for our original home beyond the stars. While the seeds of enlightenment were teaching the aborigines how to manipulate the physical stuff of life for material comfort and gain, it was also conveying to them a sense of mission to teach all sentient beings that the physical level must be transcended, that evolution must be ever toward the Source, that progress must be an odyssey back to the stars.

I have a sense of being extremely long-lived, according to Earth years. I see each generation of Earthlings with whom we interact become taller of stature, keener of brain, more compassionate of heart, more appreciative of beauty, more aware of the evils of injustice, exploitation, and cruelty. And with each successive generation, the seeds of wisdom transmit gifts of the spirit—telepathy, prophecy, healing—and memories of another world, a better place, a utopian society, a heaven. Those who bear the Starseed within them truly become as "giants in the Earth."

I have seen an entity whom I somehow know is the physical expression of my Soul at that moment in space and time, standing with his arm around a golden-haired woman with large golden eyes, whom I somehow feel is Francie's expression of Soul at that time.

I say, "My dearest, our seedlings are growing all over the planet, among all of their tribes and their peoples. Our seeds of wisdom and unconditional love have given them the creative potential to be as gods."

I move my arms around her, enjoying the feeling of flesh warmth. When she speaks it is in a voice as musical and evocative as a flute softly played at sunset:

"I pray that we have done the right thing, my dear one. Until they learn balance and control of the energies around them, their creativity will always be of low degree in their material plane. I fear they may create only chaos and yield to the discordant polarity."

I move closer to her flesh warmth. "That is why we shall always be with them, to guide them, to direct them. When we can no longer express ourselves physically, when we have evolved to a higher plane of existence, we shall be with them in their dreams, their visions, and through projected telepathy."

It seems as though the above past life may be archetypal in nature, identifying, as I do, with the Starseed Sowers within the context of the vision.

It may also be that it is in the nature of a teaching vision, which seeks to explain more of the Star People mythos to me.

The alleged past life did not truly manifest itself until our research began in earnest in 1975, so I would have to concede that the inner experience may be a reaction to the subject matter with which Francie and I were beginning to concern ourselves on a daily basis.

Briefly, at this point, I will describe the vision which Francie received which explains the true nature of the Soul in regard to past lives [a more complete description may be found in *The Star People*].

Francie was shown a golden, glowing sphere, which she understood to represent the accumulated energy frequencies of her Soul. In a flash of insight, which quickly overlayed the image of the glowing sphere, she saw that her Soul was connected in a remarkable network to an inestimable number of other Souls and that all of the Souls were attached by a lifeline to the Source of All That Is.

Extending from the Soul-sphere were many fine threads which connected smaller, crystallike balls to the central hub. These delicate "umbilical cords" fastened each lifeform that the Soul had experienced in a starburst pattern around itself.

She watched an embryo forming within each of the crystal

spheres, saw them become children, then mature to various ages. As the lifeforms matured, they gathered knowledge, experience, growings—all which were represented by tiny blue lights sparkling around the individual crystals. Corresponding lights also were transmitted to the central Soul-sphere, and its brilliance grew with each reception of energy.

Francie knew that the vibrations of love, wisdom, and knowledge, gathered by each physical expression of Soul, were feeding the central sphere. She knew that, as the lights in the individual crystals dimmed, the vision was showing her the fleshly deaths of the lifeforms.

The vision was telling her that Souls progressed in such a fashion, gathering vibrations from their physical expressions, until they raised their own energies with the various awarenesses gained by the lifeforms. The goal of each Soul was to return to the Highest Vibration, the Source of All That Is, in a frequency more enriched, more pure and true, than when it was first created and sent forth to enter the dimension of experience.

A man's face appeared in one of the balls around the central Soul-sphere. Francie's own form manifested itself in another crystal. Dozens of other men and women materialized, with faces of various colors, various ethnic backgrounds—yet all were facets of physical expression emanating from one central Soul-sphere. All were previous manifestations of Francie's Soul energy in physical form.

On another occasion when I was exploring my own past lives, I discovered another existence which I am quite certain that I experienced with Francie. I received a distinct impression that we had lived a life together in Egypt during the reign of Akhenaten, who championed the cause of monotheism 3300 Earth years ago. Francie was a lady of the palace at Akhet-Aten. I was an officer in the Pharaoh's armies.

I clearly saw images of a woman whom I felt to be Francie in stylized wig and aristocratic gown, a pet leopard at her side. The expression of her Soul's physicality in Egypt bore little resemblance to the Francie I know, yet I recognized her eyes and the essence of her.

I perceived myself wearing the headdress and uniform of my rank, and it was apparent that I lived as boldly as I strode through the fields of battle. Neither did I resemble my present fleshly materialization, but my essence of Soul somehow identified me.

In this alleged Soul memory, Francie and I had been lovers who had foresworn marriage until the belief of Akhenaten became accepted by all of Egypt. But such widespread acceptance was not to be. The two idealists were slain, together with thousands of others, as heretics against the old gods when the persecutions broke out after Akhenaten's death.

The strangest of all memories suggestive of past lives which I have received concerning Francie and myself has me as an alchemist or wizard who lives deep in the woods but who serves a powerful lord. One night under a full moon I come across this mysterious creature with strangely slanted eyes, long black hair, and very dark complexion. I feel a compelling mixture of fear and fascination, and an overwhelming state of sexual arousal.

On the third night of the full moon and on the third night of our secretive meetings, we make love in the tall grasses next to a river. That is when I notice that the long, black hair covers strangely pointed ears. The large, dark, slanted eyes look up at me appraisingly. I sense that to give evidence of fear could mean my death. I continue to make love to her, knowing within that I have the ability to control the creature's moods and to learn much arcane wisdom from her.

My mysterious forest creature becomes my wife, teaching me secrets beyond my wildest imaginings. I become highly respected as the most accomplished wizard in the kingdom, yet all credit is due my mute wife, who never speaks a word, but who, somehow, "talks" to me inside my head. I grow old, but she does not.

My last memory in that life experience is the sight of tears forming in corners of the slanted eyes as I transcend the physical body.

Yes, I know. The alleged memory is a bizarre one, but it has surfaced numerous times in my personal past-life explorations and at both odd and intimate moments during the years of Francie's and my relationship.

The most powerful memories of a past life together were shared by each of us before we even met in our present life experiences.

Ever since I was a young boy I have had fleeting images

of having been a Spanish knight. In one of the most memorable scenes, I remember sitting astride my horse, observing a picturesque cottage in the woods. Screams alert me to behold a blonde girl in a peasant blouse and dark skirt running to escape a great, bearded lout, who is chasing her on horseback. I intervene and slay the brutish man.

When Francie and I met, we had an instantaneous Soul recognition on several levels. Then, incredibly, I found myself saying, "You were the blonde girl in the forest."

Francie blinked back her astonishment, then smiled and nodded. "And you were the knight who saved me."

Remarkably, numerous psychic sensitives have recalled the scene quite independently of one another. In widely separated sections of the country, psychically talented men and women have told us how "Brad was a knight who saved Francie from being molested by a big, bearded brute of a man."

As we came together as man and woman, so did a more complete past-life attunement arrange the fragments of memory into a more coherent story.

The scene was in the Pyrenees mountain region. We were members of the Albigensian sect living in Béziers when Pope Innocent III launched a crusade against the city over seven hundred years ago. Francie was a seeress who lived in a cottage in the forest. I was a Spanish nobleman who had spoken out against the Holy Roman Church and had fled across the Pyrenees to join the Albigensians.

In that lifetime, Francie's Soul embodiment was a channel for Higher Intelligences, just as she is today. She was in constant communication with an angel, who guided her then, as he does in her present Soul experience.

"Don Ricardo" saved "Francesca," the lovely witch of the woods, from a brutal attack by a knight who had forsaken his vows of chastity. The two became inseparable from that moment to their deaths—his, defending the walls of Béziers against the Pope's armies; hers, by execution when the walls fell.

Not long ago, I received the following communication during my time in the Silence:

*In these times of transition, the seed within you is a protection, because it provides you with the knowing that you are the citizen of more than one level of being, more than one dimensional essence, more than one universe. You and Francie have been brought together once again, because those who have the knowledge of the seed within should be blended in work units.*

*You must understand that certain of the Starseed are as vibrational "sponges" or "balancers." These bearers of our seed are scattered among humankind for the literal purpose of absorbing negativity. Francie is one of these sponges, and she will very much need your strength and your balance in the coming days of transformation which lie ahead for your species.*

*When two or more Starseed come together, they become a living vessel which contains both the physical and the spiritual expression of that energy which you understand best as the Christ energy or the Christ consciousness. This energy, and so much more, will be granted to you when you have received initiation according to the inner teachings now being transmitted to all evolutionized Earthlings.*

*Until such time, you must remain positive at all times. You must accept that whatever happens to you is a learning experience for your good and your gaining. You must understand that all life is a quest, and that a positive attitude maintained during the striving is of equal importance to your attaining the goal.*

*Banish fear from your life. Energies draw their corresponding polarities, like the poles of a magnet. Fears draw negativities. Fears open the polarized door very widely and attract malignant thoughtforms.*

*All those who bear the seed within them have the liberating knowledge that multidimensional beings of light exist to guide them.*

*The awareness of the externality of the Soul, the gift of unconditional love, and the potential of controlling powerful Earth-energies will permit the Starseed and certain highly evolutionized Earthlings to become as gods on the creative level of the Earth plane.*

*When the seed within permits humankind to attain such self-mastery, all elements now considered evil, hostile, or chaotic will be rendered totally powerless.*

# Chapter Four

## ALIEN MEMORIES

As the seed bursts, the galaxy is born; and as thought glows,
a cosmos comes to be.

*Roger W. Wescott*


A few years ago, during our past-lives consultations, Francie
and I, together with other researchers, began to discover increasing numbers of men and women who, during altered-states
regressions, claimed to have memories of having lived previous
life experiences on other worlds or dimensions. For a time, it
seemed as though about one person in five who came to us for
a consultation relived an alien lifetime while undergoing regressions. In other instances, the people had come to us because
of dreams and apparent memory flashes of life on other planets.

Basically, the subjects with whom we worked fit into one
of three general categories which I had discovered in earlier
research in the late 1960s and early '70s. Since one is always
somewhat excited to receive corroboration of previous data, I
found myself bringing old files out of the cabinets and blending
prior information with the new material which we were receiving. The three general categories of claimed alien memories

are those which I have termed the "Refugees," the "Utopians," and the "Energy Essences."

The Refugee Alien scenario surfaced from the regressed men and women who claimed memories of having come to Earth after they had fled their native planet because of great civil wars or cataclysmic natural disasters.

In some cases, they seemed to recall having come to this planet on a kind of reconnaissance mission and crash-landed here. In any case, the aliens ended up trapped on Earth, unable to return to their home planet.

The regressed subjects described themselves as humanlike in appearance, and we found that their stories blended in many ways with our Star People concepts.

The Utopians seemed to form the largest category among our subjects. These aliens appeared to be deliberate planetary colonizers who erected their space domes wherever they traveled in memory of the lifestyle on their world of origin. They were themselves dome-headed, suggestive of a highly evolved brain capacity, and were similar in all recognizable aspects to *Homo sapiens sapiens*.

These aliens could also have served as the direct ancestors of many of our subjects. I labeled them "Utopians" because their descriptions of their social and political structures seemed so idealistically perfect.

The Energy Essences were the strangest of all. Entranced men and women spoke of existences as disembodied entities of pure energy, yet with awareness. In a sense, they were mind-essences which were able to exist on even inhospitable, barren planets—or in space itself.

In my opinion, these entities were not at all to be confused with angelic intelligences. In many cases, these essences drifted rather purposelessly through space. In other instances, they approached specific planets with the intention of inhabiting already existing physical bodies.

As I suggested, we gained the most information about the Utopians. We heard of a planet with a reddish sky and with two moons. The cities and the individual homes were described as having been of crystal or some material which was crystalline in effect. The buildings appeared translucent for the most part, but we also heard descriptions of the sun reflecting off spires

# THE SEED

and turrets. We were often told that the cities were sheltered under protective domes.

The subjects who recalled lives as Utopians under altered-states regression expressed a great nostalgia for the culture of that lost planet. The cities seemed to be run according to the ideals of a perfect democracy. Citizens enjoyed total freedom without the harsh byproducts of civilization—crime, hunger, poverty.

A family unit in the manner that we know it did not seem to exist. Communal living, of a sort, seemed to prevail, although each person had his individual space and privacy.

Numerous subjects testified that the Utopians ate very sparingly, most often of a concentrated food that was made into a souplike mixture. The culture was completely vegetarian with no flesh foods of any kind being consumed.

Our subjects most often remembered themselves as slender, quite short, with big-domed heads. Although they had little body hair and no beards or mustaches, they did mention longish golden hair and eyelashes. Their skin was most often said to be of golden brown complexion, and their eyes were of a similar color.

While under trance, we had several subjects begin to speak in a musical babble of language, which sounded very much like a cross between humming and talking in a singsong accent with a lot of "1s" and "ms" blended harmoniously. The Utopians had names like "Muma," Lee-la," "Lu-ah."

Music seemed to be an intrinsic element in their culture, and we were told that it was primarily a free-form, nonrepetitive sound that often became a part of their thoughts.

In contrast to the tranquil, gentle lives of the Utopians, the Refugees' regressions were filled with accounts of violent civil wars, burning cities, global holocausts. Many reported that they had fled the planet before it exploded.

The accounts of a beleaguered, dying planet began to sound so reminiscent of tales of the legendary Atlantis that I speculated whether or not that memory which seemed so indelibly etched in humankind's collective unconscious might not have actually occurred on another planet light years away in space.

Although the Refugees were generally less able to provide us with the kind of detailed information about their culture which the Utopians had given us, we found a number of these subjects concerned with the recall of antigravity devices, cancer cures, fireproofing formulas, and other advantages of their advanced technology.

Most of their memories, however, were cluttered with survival thoughts and plans of escape from their doomed world. We did eventually manage to work with a number of subjects who seemed to have shared lives in the priestcraft of a temple on this planet, but they, too, remembered more of the destruction of the building than their daily rituals.

Most typical of the Refugee regressions were graphic descriptions of immense portions of their planet being ripped apart by explosions and large numbers of the population being annihilated. We also recorded several subjects describing fiery crash landings on Earth or on other planets, as their war-damaged spacecraft failed to negotiate proper landings.

At this point in our research, it would seem appropriate to add a fourth category to our alien memories. We have heard from increasingly large numbers of Star People who claim to recall coming to Earth for the express purpose of assuming incarnations on the planet as part of an extended mission of raising the level of humankind's consciousness.

Typical of such reports is the one sent to us by A.M., a schoolteacher from Westminster, Colorado:

> In this dream, I am in a place of great (but no blinding) light. Other "beings" are there, although I cannot remember anything of their actual physical appearance.
>
> It seems that we are in a rather large, round object which hovers a short distance above Earth. I am being shown a chutelike passageway leading downward, and I am given to understand that I am to go through this chute.
>
> My feelings about descending are not those of joy, but more like necessity or duty. This all seems to be part of the Plan. My last awareness is of passing downward...toward the Earth. There is no feeling of threat or danger, merely some sadness at separation from the other beings. The dream ends. The images remain.

A woman secretary in the California school district, who is also an amateur filmmaker, informed us that she "remembered" volunteering to come here on assignment from Galactic Command. Her role was to be that of one of a group of counselors who would assist Earth to evolve spiritually. On her planet of origin, she was a scientist who worked with channeling light as a source of energy.

According to her alien memories, her first life experience on Earth occurred in the Yucatán, where she was regarded as an oracle and where, for a time, she experimented with hypnotic drugs, which had been carefully devised to enable the native people to establish closer telepathic contact with her.

Jay of Windsor, Ontario, has his Ph.D. in Educational Psychology, and a belief in reincarnation to help explain in a balanced way the "strange things" which occurred to him as a youth:

I understand that this is my first incarnation on Earth and that I volunteered to embark upon a specific mission, now nearing the completion of its first phase. I seem to remember, also, that I have a personal achievement to complete—that of learning patience. I always see myself in the past as an ethereal, rather than material, being.

It is my understanding that it is my mission to discover and to develop the skills needed to help my fellow human beings, whether they are *homo sapiens* or *homo astrolis*, to "overcome," whatever this last word means.

I also understand that I now have two parts of a three-part puzzle.

The first part involves the fundamental importance of the ways we perceive reality. These perceptions, the operation of which we are largely unaware, can serve to help or to hinder our progress, depending on whether or not they reveal or mask our true pathways.

The second aspect relates to the ways in which we apply our perceptions, as a build-up of others or as a put-down of them or ourselves. Considerable skill is needed here, since put-downs are often subtle and overtly unintentional.

I can only guess, at this point, the basis of the third part. I have been told to work on these two for a while, to get their details, and that the third will come. With the third, the golden chain will be complete and the window will open. . . .

Another Star Person from Ontario, a thirty-two-year-old man, stated that he can recall each of his five previous lifetimes on this planet, and in each prior existence he has served as a contact point for UFO intelligences:

On my native planet, I was a dream interpreter. I was sent to Earth to help prepare Earthlings for the coming UFO contact on a global basis.

I lived in a city of light, of crystal buildings, where everything was peace and harmony. I used dreams to interpret any forthcoming health problems and to help people better understand themselves. We had conquered pain and suffering by our mental abilities—and these are gifts that we will one day be able to give to Earthlings.

Interestingly, we have heard from a number of Cherokee Indians who seem to fit into this fourth category of aliens on assignments of raising Earth awareness. I know of several psychic sensitives, including Francie, who bear the Cherokee heritage within them as a part of their genetic composition.

A Cherokee physicist, who now lives in Alabama, not only had recall of a past life in the Pleiades, but he was also able to fit his alien memories together with tribal legends that his people had come from another world:

We lived in domed cities with translucent walls. We could fly, communicate with animals, transport ourselves instantly to other parts of our world.

I remember our city as a golden color—a place of great beauty and calm.

I came with others from my planet to help Earth through its birth pains into an intergalactic community and one-ness. We were members of the priestcraft in ancient Egypt; we were alchemists in the Middle Ages; we are scientists and clergy in the modern world.

The whole matter of sensible men and women who claim alien memories invites extensive speculation.

Are these people, because of their higher intelligence and greater sensitivity, rejecting an association with Earth because of all the inadequacies and shortcomings which they witness all around them?

Does the mechanism of believing oneself to be of alien heritage enable one to deal more objectively with the multitude of problems which assail the conscientious and caring at every dawn of a new day?

But why do the alleged memories surface at such early ages? Why do these men and women recall an awareness of their "true home" long before they have begun to confront the harsh realities of successful existence on the planet?

"I am thirty-two years old," writes Linda of Yonkers, New York. "And I have lived most of the first sixteen thinking that I was crazy, because I always knew that I was from another world."

Linda, a nurse who has recently left formal medicine so that she might become a spiritual healer, related the following experiences:

My earliest recollection was at the age of five. I was at our country house. It's something I have never forgotten. For some reason I was very upset. I remember standing on the very top of my slide, looking up at the night sky.... I was just about hysterical as I looked up toward space. Through my tears I remember screaming:

"Come back, please! Don't leave me here with these barbarians. Why am I being punished so? This is not my home. These are not my people!"

I had an awareness that my people were leaving me behind. My world was the planet Orion.

Today, when Linda's longing for Home becomes unbearable, she goes to their house in upstate New York where there are many fir trees:

To me, the fir tree is sacred. There are two places that I go to where the trees form a circle, and I sit or stand in the middle. I can feel the spirit of the trees reach out to hold and comfort me, as if they knew my plight.

Linda is fortunate in that her husband, she writes, is very understanding of her beliefs:

He now knows and sincerely believes that I am an alien. I've told him about my past lives on this world and my lives on other worlds.

I have met a few . . . like myself, but only one remains in contact. The others are finding it very difficult to cope with their memories of our true Home.

A woman named Monica remembers being a scientist from another world who participated in creating the first crude [*Homo sapiens*] of this world.

Apparently, in this scientific work she did, she was cruel to these creatures.

But something happened. She realized these creatures had feelings.

I'll never forget how she looked when she told me how one of the creatures had taken her hand one day and caressed it. Monica realized then that just because one may have the knowledge to create a lifeform, it doesn't give one the right to *abuse* a lifeform.

In 1975, Linda wrote a poem which expressed many of her feelings of being an alien living on Earth:

I remember as if it were yesterday. Three ships approaching Earth—one burning as it entered the atmosphere, our people dying. Were they the lucky ones?

A voyage into time to save our planet. That was why we came here. So few of us are left, but we are so close, so very close to accomplishing our task. . . .

. . . My heart cries for these people and for this Earth, for there is so much agony they have yet to go through.

This world is not like the Home; it has no opal ice mountains, nor orange lakes nor unicorns. . . .

. . . This world knows so much beauty, but man has chosen to destroy it and himself.

. . . Earth man will not conquer space. But in time the Gods will descend to walk with man.

Erin, an actress who lives in Burbank, interprets her memories as indicators that she is a member of a Council on Humanities in Space Command—although she does recognize that such alleged recollections could be symbolical. In either event, she has long been drawn to the Pleiades, and she expressed her fascination in the following poem:

> I am drawn
> > to
> the fiery triangle
> > of starlight
> nourished by its
> > mother force
> from whence
> > my spark ignited.
>
> I was sent forth
> > to light the way
> > > for other
> stars of journeys predestined.

Judy of Amarillo, Texas, told us that she had waited all of her thirty-eight years for such research as ours to be made public, for "somebody else to say what I've always known."

In a poem which she entitles, "The Knowledge," Judy says

> I am alien to your land.
> Not by virtue of miles, state, or country:
> But by the inner and outer timelessness
> you define as space...
>
> ...I am not alone here: There are others who
> share the loneliness, the emptiness, the
> Knowledge.
>
> ...I gaze skyward, answering the Infinite's
> recall.
> If to be lost here is to die,
> then to die here is not lost.
>
> For I shall rejoin the Great Spiral,
> and that will take me Home.

Karen of Bricktown, New Jersey, identified herself to us as a "Starbaby." When she was seventeen, she set down thoughts which defined her differentness from her friends:

I wasn't born here. My body must have been, but my soul and my mind are not of Earth. . . . It's almost as if two different beings are housed beneath my skull—the human part functioning just about all of the time; the alien part taking control but for a second or two, then disappearing once again into the background. But in that split second, I see more, know more, than I have ever seen or known in a lifetime.

Today, Karen's professional status places her in customer service, and she genuinely feels best when she knows that she truly is helping someone. Although she used to torment herself with thoughts of whether she was a weed among the flowers or a flower among the weeds, she declared that it was now "fantastic" to finally understand (after reading *The Star People*) that she was "*not* nuts!"

A Massachusetts social worker, a woman of Irish and French ancestry, told us her memories of having lived on a planet called "Xantho." The entities there were basically humanlike in appearance, spoke a language known as Sumar, and sent emissaries to Earth to design the pyramids. According to this Star Person, the pyramids were "transmitters of an energy system known as 'Usan.'"

The social worker went on to inform us of her recollection of having been sent to Earth by a "Council of Twelve."

According to her thoughts, "We were responsible for the miracles recorded in the book of *Exodus*. We parted the Red Sea. Our craft created the columns of fire and of smoke which led the Israelites. We rained manna from the skies to feed the wandering tribes, and we even located water for them, cracking apart the ground to cause it to well up."

A forty-three-year-old industrial consultant from Arkansas vividly recalled his life as a "starcraft engineer" who was on board a vehicle that was forced to crash-land on Earth during an expedition to gather raw materials for industrial processing.

All our systems were failing, and the pilots could barely keep the craft under control. We had lost most of our drive system, and we were preparing to die in the impact of the crash. . . . My readouts were going mad, and when

I glanced out the porthole, I could see the surface of Earth approaching.

After the crash-landing—in what is now northern Europe—we discovered that the pilots had managed to touch down with only minor damage. But, tragically, although the engineering crew worked for months to attempt a repair, we could not get us spaceborne again. We couldn't even get our emergency signals to muster up enough strength to have a chance to rescue.

I died in what is now Germany, and I lived several lifetimes on Earth prior to my present existence. I feel trapped here. I still want to get back to my home planet.

Journalist Paul Bannister, intrigued by our research with men and women who recalled alien memories under altered-states regression or during dreams and visions, interviewed other paranormal researchers to learn how common such experiences might be.

Frederick Lenz, former professor of philosophy and author of the book, *Lifetimes: True Accounts of Reincarnation*, told him that out of about one thousand people whom he has regressed, several hundred had described life on other worlds.

Dr. Edith Fiore, a clinical psychologist and hypnotherapist from Saratoga, California, author of *You Have Been Here Before: A Psychologist Looks at Past Lives*, told Bannister that she was convinced that some of her patients had lived before as aliens on other planets. What is more, she informed the journalist, she had been able to use certain data provided by such memories to cure her subjects of health or other problems.

Dr. Fiore recounted the case of a man, a nuclear engineer, who had great difficulty memorizing things. Under hypnosis, it was revealed that the man had been a spacecraft pilot who had been assigned to transport a group of people from one planet to another. On one particular flight, he had been dismayed to learn, the craft designated for his use was an outdated model. Disgruntled, he flew it anyway, against his better judgment.

"He directed the craft by mental projections," Dr. Fiore stated. "And at a critical time, a small child who was emotionally upset came to him from the passenger area. Because he was paying her attention, he forgot vital mental commands. He was forced to crash-land in a desert on Earth, and, during a trek to find water, both he and all his passengers died of thirst."

In spite of the tragic ending of that previous life experience, Dr. Fiore reported, she was able to use that knowledge "to help him remember things again—a direct application of past-life therapy."

The clinical psychologist told Bannister that she agreed with our findings, even though she had not yet acquired the data base that we had.

She said that her patients had recalled living in enclosed cities on other worlds. They had spoken of domed cities with ramps and space buggies.

Dr. Fiore further stated that she was familiar with the kind of descriptions that we had amassed "of smooth, golden-skinned people with blond hair smaller than we are."

She also admitted that she had often heard subjects complain of feeling foreign, alien, here on Earth. "I would not be surprised to find that we all have had lives on other planets," Dr. Fiore said.

And if one accepts the eternality of the Soul and its evolutionary progression, why must such a return to the Source of All That Is be limited to physical expressions lived only on the planet Earth?

If one accepts one God-Intelligence for the universe, why should each Soul not experience that Divine handiwork wherever it manifests itself?

If one accepts a progression of lifetimes as opportunities for growth and for learning, why should we be confined only to the "classrooms" of planet Earth?

Dr. Leo Sprinkle, director of counseling services at the University of Wyoming and an internationally acclaimed authority on past-life regressions of UFO encounters, told Bannister that he had found "significant past-life experiences" on other planets.

"Although we cannot prove that it is true," Dr. Sprinkle admitted, "I am convinced that it is possible that some people have lived before as aliens. One other possibility is that these memories have been implanted in order to program us to prepare for life off this planet."

Professor Sprinkle estimated that among the five hundred subjects whom he had regressed, a small "but significant" number had reported prior life experiences on other planets. He had heard of the red sky and the two moons from several patients. He had also listened to accounts of crystal cities and translucent buildings.

Academically cautious, Dr. Sprinkle was confident enough of his research to tell Bannister that such alien memories fit with the patterns of his patients' present lives: "These recollections are vivid and powerful, and I believe that these people are being sincere when they say these were their past lives. I have one woman who feels very angry. She feels she has been trapped here on Earth, and she just wants to get off the planet and return home."

Dr. Sprinkle went on to say that most of the people whom he had regressed considered themselves to be part of a larger system, part of a larger order.

The psychologist admitted to Bannister that he had participated in our original survey of Star People. Although he does not consider himself to be Starseed, Dr. Sprinkle does feel that he might have a role to play as a helper, "to usher in a New Age when science and religion will come together."

Dr. Sprinkle is of the opinion that we should consider the enigma of alien memories from various standpoints:

> If we don't like the hypothesis that we have been seeded from extraterrestrial beings, we can still accept the hypothesis that somebody—our own subconscious, God, higher beings, *somebody*—is encouraging us to think in terms of space travel. We may be undergoing a process of mental programming by intelligent beings to provide us with guidelines so that in the future our children or our grandchildren will be able to go to other worlds.

And perhaps equally profound as a mental conditioning process are the dreams and memories which have been reported to us from men and women who claim to recall experiences aboard UFOs.

Whether it was a dream or an actual experience on some level of reality, Ruth of Anchorage, Alaska, clearly remembers "being taken into a very large room with a high ceiling in a kind of city-ship, where I was shown large, high, clear cylinders of various plants and animals."

Her other undiminished memory is of being "at a control panel in a space ship. It was night and dark within the ship except for a kind of red glow around the instrument panel.

"I was shown the lights of Earth below," she continues, "and I felt thrilled and amazed. This was in 1945 in Puyallup, Washington. I was not afraid of my 'hosts.' Instead, after that, I often sent them telepathic messages to come back and take me with them, pointing out that there were fields on our farm where they could land safely without being seen."

In what could have been a dream, an out-of-body experience, or an actual encounter, Geoffrey of Bradford, Pennsylvania, remembers being awakened by a "brilliant, flickering light pouring in through the gaps of the window blind. It pulsed and flickered in time to a weird, fluttering, whirring or buzzing sound."

Succumbing at first to fear, Geoffrey then became aware of an entity in his room:

> I knew that I was what the brilliantly luminous being had come for. I wanted to run. Suddenly, and quite involuntarily, I was standing beside my bed, looking at the being, no longer luminous, but having assumed the form of a typical UFO humanoid, whose appearance is well-documented in the literature.

The humanoid refused to answer Geoffrey's admittedly "inane" questions, but, rather, took him by the wrists, and floated horizontally across the room, towing Geoffrey after him.

> I experienced the sensation of being "peeled" from the inside and drawn through the window. . . . Once outside, things got confused and fuzzy. . . . I was not permitted to speak, but he stated: "You are wasting your time in this camp."
> These words were followed by a bewildering series of visions centering on my friends and relatives, which seemed to comprise the "camp" to which he had referred. . . . At the end of the visional sequence, I awoke in bed. It is now almost six months later, and I have not seen the entity again.

Natalie of Milpitas, California, was contacted first by beings of light who showed her the physical reality of their spacecraft.

Then, on June 26, 1980, she once again encountered the same entities:

> They gave me a demonstration of their powers, which were awesome to say the least. They can make things appear and disappear at will. They also told me to start practicing telepathy, as I will need my *previous* abilities.
>
> I was informed the craft that I had flown in a past life had crashed to Earth because it had materialized at the wrong angle to counteract the planet's gravitational pull. I was being activated at this time in this life experience in order to help establish a direct communications link between their planet and Earth.
>
> They took me on a tour of the interior of their ship. . . . I felt that I should bow to them, but they told me not to. They said that I had once been as they now appeared to me. I got this overpowering feeling of love and goodness from them. Other beings on the ship sent me peace and love vibrations . . . The beings glowed . . . They are very advanced, but they still wish to assist us during our coming times of change.

Dianne, from Las Vegas, Nevada, sent us an account that, almost word for word, we have received with such great similarity from so many other men and women that it might appear that Francie and I have become, in one sense, archetypal figures:

> I remember being with a crowd of people in what seemed to be a space vehicle of the sort that Earth does not yet know. We were listening to Brad give us instructions pertaining to what we were to do once we had arrived at our destination. We were in a darkened room, viewing a large wall screen on which pictures of Earth appeared. Brad was briefing us concerning the planet.
>
> We in the group were chronologically younger than the teachers, although they really did not appear physically that much older. Francie stood beside Brad, and they both looked as they do now—even their hair styles were basically the same. During their instructions to us, they stood on a semi-circular platform about seven feet high, so we could see and hear them clearly.

The next report is also familiar to me, and its implications, if one will permit oneself to consider them, are quite staggering. Shortly after Doriel of Chicago, Illinois, had seen a UFO, two beings appeared to her:

> Rather, I could feel their presence and hear them. One, a female, was named Leita or Leia. The other, a male, was named Gamal. They told me that they wanted to incarnate through me. I was around eleven at the time.
>
> I asked them, why me? They told me because I was one of them. They said that I could provide the right environment for them.
>
> I have a daughter now. I gave her Leita for her middle name. I was told six months before I became pregnant that a child would be coming to me. I practiced Tantric Yoga exercises prenatally and had natural childbirth.
>
> After she was born, I told her what solar system she was in, which galaxy, and that I would be her guardian. Physiologically speaking, I had been told that I would be unable ever to become pregnant.

This last account leads us directly into the next chapter. Sometime in 1975, Karen of Grand Rapids, Michigan, dreamed that she heard a voice coming from the hill behind her house:

> I got up and put on my robe and followed the voice that was calling my name. I walked over the hill, and in the field behind it was a UFO, a very large one. I saw three figures standing beside it. I walked up to them, but I could say nothing. I felt they had control over me.
>
> They explained why they were there and why they wanted me. They wanted me to give birth to one of their kind. I had been selected because I was of their kind, also.
>
> One of the three men, who was standing on my right, came up to me and slowly started slipping off my robe. I tried to move, but I could not. The man on my left stepped forward and started touching me. All I could do was cry. They told me that they would not hurt me, so I should not worry.
>
> As they helped me with my robe, I could hear them speaking to me. Their mouths were not moving, so I

knew that they were using telepathy. They told me that I could go back and that they would be contacting me at a later time. The next thing I knew, I was at my patio door. [In her communication to us, Karen added that her daughter, who was by then five years old, had been observed levitating. She also spoke intimately of relatives deceased before her birth, and she had already outlined her future life as a healer in a hospital.]

These men were dark complexioned with slightly slanted eyes. They were small of build and stood about five feet to five-feet-four inches tall. They wore a two-piece suit with a belt around the waist. They had boots on their feet with their pants' legs tucked inside. On their belt buckles they had some sort of symbol. It looked like some kind of bird in flight.

Could not that birdlike symbol have been a representation of a flying serpent?

I think so. And I recall the sketches of winged serpents which have been drawn by those UFO contactees whom I have placed under hypnotic regression.

In numerous sessions over the past fourteen years, I have seen that serpentine symbol, that insignia of aerial command, appear far more times than the laws of chance could ever permit.

And in each instance, I have remembered the small, serpent-eyed entity who visited our farm that October night in 1940.

# Chapter Five

## REPTILIAN GENESIS

Old tides pull at me and ancient swells sweep in from forgotten seas...and there is a star in the southern sky, the most magnificent star that I have ever seen, and I am beginning to know its name....

*Robert Ardrey*

The veteran archaeologist who stood above the dig in the San Francisco mountains, near the Hopi community of Old Oraibi in northern Arizona, knew that the skeleton of the Indian woman and the remains of the strange, unborn child within her could rewrite the history of the human race.

He turned up the collar of his wool jacket against the chill wind. Flagstaff was about to get its first snowfall of the season. The wind began to whistle and to hum eerily through the needles of the swaying ponderosa pines, and the mournful sound reminded him of a Navajo burial chant that he had once heard.

They had found the skeleton of the woman first. It appeared as though she had been covered by a cave-in next to a river. The trouble was, as one of his students had pointed out, there had been no rivers or sand there for thousands of years.

He had agreed. There had been no rivers there for about

25,000 years. There had been a wet period before that time, with inner-mountain basin damming and flooding. The trouble was, there weren't supposed to be any Indians there until much later.

Excitedly, they dug away sand and bits of shell. They even found charcoal traces, as if she had been sitting near a fire when the cave-in had occurred.

The skeleton had bits of leather clothing stuck here and there to the upper torso. A few beads still adhered to the crisp and curled shreds of animal flesh.

The skull and its teeth appeared prototypically Amerindian.

It was when the students had dug deeper that they had drawn back from the trench in a kind of horror, as if they had violated a most sacred place. It was now apparent that the woman had died in childbirth. Her pelvis was fractured, and the bones of the infant that had sought release from her uterine harbor were still lying there amidst the shards of the broken skeletal nest.

They had been stunned by the size of the unborn baby's head. "Mongoloid," the enthusiastic students had speculated. "Down's syndrome."

Kneeling cautiously next to the skeletal remains of the baby and working carefully with brushes and picks, the archaeologist counted thirty-five, rather than the normal thirty-three vertebrae; fourteen pairs of ribs, rather than the usual twelve; and only three fingers, with abnormally long digits.

Not only was the skull extraordinarily large, but it was elongated in a peculiar manner. And no one could stop discussing the unusually large, and peculiarly slanted, eye sockets.

Later, while the students were preparing some lunch, the archaeologist discovered that the jaws of the infant skull already contained a set of perfectly formed baby teeth. What was more astonishing, they were not the typical Amerindian dentition. They did not have the markedly scooped-out, shovel-shaped incisors that they should have had if the child were Amerindian. And their surfaces were simpler and smoother than that of modern humans, totally devoid of pits and fissures, as if designed for an exclusively vegetarian diet.

What had they found in this rude and informal grave near Old Oraibi, the oldest continually occupied village in North America?

Was the baby a freak of nature—or something much more significant than a spontaneous distortion of genetics?

Before the archaeologist unveiled the skeletal Madonna and child to any board of academicians, he had to have some answers to some very perplexing questions.

First, he had to deal with the apparent antiquity of the find. Since it appeared that the bones had been found *in situ* with geologic strata indicative of 30,000 years or more, he had to explain how an Indian woman in travail had come to be in a place where she should not have been.

Second, he had to explain how an unconventional infant had come to be in the process of emerging from a conventional womb. An infant who was so unconventional that he appeared as though he might have been sired by a father from another species—or another world.

The scene just described has not yet occurred, but I am convinced that one day it shall.

In the late 1960s, I participated in the hypnotic regression of a number of men and women who claimed to have been abducted for brief periods of time by crew members from UFOs. These contactees claimed to have been given some kind of medical examination; and in some instances, we were able to observe peculiar punctures and markings in their flesh.

I interviewed even larger numbers of witnesses who claimed to have seen UFOnauts in the vicinity of mysterious craft that had been set down in pastures, meadows, and forest lands. These men and women said that they had been able to get a good look at the entities, who were often engaged in such tasks as digging in the soil, clipping leaves from bushes, or taking samples of water.

In the greatest number of alien encounters, the UFOnauts were described as standing about five feet tall and dressed in one-piece, tight-fitting jumpsuits.

Their skin was gray or grayish green, and hairless.

Their faces were dominated by large eyes, very often with snakelike, slit pupils.

They had no discernable lips, just straight lines for mouths.

They seldom were described as having noses, just little snubs if at all; but usually the witness saw only nostrils nearly flush against the smooth face.

Sometimes a percipient mentioned pointed ears, but on many occasions commented on the absence of noticeable ears on the large, round head. And, repeatedly, the witnesses described an insignia of a flying serpent on a shoulder patch, a badge, a medallion, or a helmet.

It has seemed to me for years now that the UFOnauts are reptilian or amphibian humanoids, and I believe that they have been interacting with Earth for millions of years.

An archaeological enigma with which I dealt extensively in an earlier work (*Mysteries of Time and Space*) has to do with what appear to be humanoid footprints which are found widely scattered in the geologic strata suggestive of a quarter of a billion years ago. This "What's-it That Walked Like a Man" left shoe prints, sandal prints, and barefoot prints on sands of time that have long since hardened into rock. This bipedal creature with humanlike stride ostensibly vanished—and left a riddle which has the scientists scratching their heads.

Quoting from that previous book:

There must be one or more fossil animals about which science as yet knows nothing. Maybe the evolutionists have been looking up the wrong tree when they conduct their endless search for the Missing Link. Is it impossible to consider a giant, toadlike amphibian emerging from the Paleozoic swamps and pressing a foot that bore a heel and five toes on the mud and sand? An intelligent species of amphibian would be remarkably effective creatures. They could have the best of two worlds, land and sea. They could hibernate for long periods of time, whenever necessary; and, of course, they would be naturally long-lived.

To carry our amphibious fantasy a bit further, it would have been no real trick for them to have survived into the Age of Reptiles, thereby becoming responsible for those mysterious footprints in the same strata as the dinosaur tracks. The shoes? Well, if there is anything at all to evolution, the amphibians would by that time have developed a rather advanced civilization—one that would have run its course by the time an intelligent species of mammal was prepared to assume stage center.

These footprints were made more than 250 million years ago. That is a great deal of time for trial and error, but also an enormous stretch of time for other kinds of intelligent species to flower and die.

In numerous lectures throughout the United States and Canada, I have presented my hypothesis that the reason why the most frequently reported UFOnauts resemble reptilian humanoids may be because that is exactly what they are—highly evolved members of a serpentine species.

My thesis is willing to entertain two possibilities:

(1)The amphibians evolved into a humanoid species that eventually developed a culture that ran its course or was destroyed in an Atlantis-type catastrophe—just after they had begun exploring extraterrestrial frontiers. Today's UFOnauts, then, may be the descendents of the survivors of that amphibian culture returning from their space colony to monitor the present dominant species on the home planet.

(2)Today's UFOnauts may, in fact, be a highly advanced reptilian humanoid culture from an extraterrestrial world, who evolved into the dominant species on their planet millions of years ago—and who have interacted in our world's evolution as explorers, genetic engineers, and observers.

I was delighted to read newspaper articles about Dale Russell and Ron Seguin of Canada's National Museum of Natural Sciences at Ottawa, who, in their imaginative model of a humanoid dinosaur, demonstrated that scientists may still be creative and adventuresome. I took heart that the technocrats and the rats-in-the-maze behaviorists had not completely taken over after all.

The February 1982 issue of *Discover* told how Russell and Seguin's project had begun as a routine, life-sized reconstruction of *Stenonychosaurus inequalis*, a small, meat-eating dinosaur that had lived near the close of the Age of Reptiles.

Russell and Seguin decided to take the exercise a few steps farther. Using *Stenonychosaurus* as the model, they fashioned a creature that might have evolved, rather than dying out with the rest of the dinosaurs, sixty-five million years ago.

The result was a strikingly manlike four-and-a-half-foot creature that Russell calls a "dinosauroid." It has a large brain, green skin, and yellow, reptilian eyes, and is said by its creators to be based on scientific speculation, not pure fantasy.

Nature has a way of filling unoccupied ecological niches with whatever evolutionary lines are available, and Russell reasons that if the mammals had not been around to evolve

(*above*) Artist Regina de Paschal's interpretation of the "dinosauroid" fashioned by Dale Russell and Ron Seguin of Canada's National Museum of Natural Sciences at Ottawa. Using *Stenonychosaurus* as a model, they structured a creature that might have evolved, rather than dying out with the rest of the dinosaurs, sixty-five million years ago.

(*left*) From the late 1960s to the present day, Brad Steiger has participated in the hypnotic regression of dozens of men and women who claim to have encountered crew members from UFOs. In the greatest number of alien confrontations, the UFOnauts were described as standing about five feet tall and dressed in one-piece, tight-fitting jumpsuits. Their skin was gray or grayish green, and hairless. Their faces were dominated by large eyes, very often with snakelike, slit pupils. They had no discernable lips, just straight lines for mouths. They seldom were described with noses, just nostrils nearly flush against the face. Sometimes a witness described the entity with pointed ears, but frequently commented on the absence of noticeable ears on the large, round head. Repeatedly, the witnesses mentioned an insignia of a flying serpent on a shoulder patch, a badge, or a medallion. Steiger theorizes that the UFOnauts are reptilian or amphibian humanoids and that they have been interacting with Earth for millions of years.

into intelligent beings through the primate line, the reptiles might have done it instead.

"There is a trend in evolution toward increasing brain size," he says, and the trend includes dinosaurs as well as mammals.

*Stenonychosaurus* had a good start, Russell believes, because it had a relatively large brain and eyes with overlapping visual fields. It also walked on two legs, and it may have had a partially opposable "thumb" on its three-clawed hand.

In the May 1982 issue of *Omni* magazine, paleontologist Russell made a few additional speculations that rang correlative bells with my earlier UFOnaut research.

For example, Russell states that they could have given the dinosauroid ears, since they are proven useful for directionality. He did not, he admits, because it made the creature look too human.

The entity that I perceived in October of 1940 did have ears. And although some percipients of UFOnauts have commented upon the entities' lack of such, the majority have reported rather substantial, pointed ears.

Interestingly, regarding the question of language, Russell theorizes that the sounds that the dinosaur man would make would be "avian rather than mammalian. . . . Their voices would be more birdlike than grunting."

Almost without exception, those men and women who have encountered UFOnauts have said that the sounds the entities made were suggestive of whistles, hummings, chirps, musical notes—all uttered in a birdlike, singsong manner.

Russell is very cautious in his suppositions and emphasizes that he is largely playing "let's pretend" when it comes to speculations about the dinosauroid's familial and societal evolutions. About the only time that he is dogmatic is when he is declaring that intelligent mammals and intelligent reptiles could not both have developed on the same planet.

Mammals, he states, would have remained at the level of insect-eating rodents. Humankind would never have existed, because the dinosaurs ". . . would have preempted the niche that has been occupied by mammals."

In addition to the scientific speculation of Russell and Seguin regarding the evolution of an earthly reptilian humanoid, motion picture audiences recently encountered an extraterrestrial with decidedly reptilian-amphibian features in Steven Spielberg's *E.T.* The smallish, pale, doughboy entities of Spielberg's previous film, *Close Encounters of the Third Kind*, were not quite right. In *E.T.*, however, the stranded extraterrestrial seems much closer to the entity of my own childhood encounter and to the reptilian-amphibian humanoids that other men and women have met in hundreds of documented incidents.

If our contemporary science cannot accept the possibility that our planet could have witnessed the evolution of intelligent amphibians or reptilians as well as human-mammalians as successive dominant species, then I will, at this time, opt to promulgate Part Two of my hypothesis: Earth has been visited for centuries by a highly advanced reptilian humanoid culture from an extraterrestrial world.

Since I do not have the credentials of Russell and Seguin, I shall probably be told that my reconstruction of events will be assessed as "pure fantasy," rather than "scientific speculation," but, be that as it may, consider the following as objectively as possible:

The serpent is almost universally recognized as a symbol of the waveform of energy, a sperm-symbol representative of life. Nearly every ancient culture has its legends of wise Serpent Kings who came from the sky to advance the beneficent and civilizing rule of the Sons of Heaven, upon Earth—e.g., Quetzalcoatl, the "feathered serpent" of the Incas, who descended from heaven in a silver egg. The awesome respect that our ancestors had for these wise serpentlike humanoids could surely have been retained in our collective unconscious today.

Let us suppose, then, that a highly advanced reptilian species with an astonishing technology has been interacting with developing lifeforms on Earth for millions of years.

Let us suppose, further, that, upon the emergence of humankind's earliest ancestral relative, they made a decision to interfere with the gradual evolutionary process of *Homo sapiens* and to initiate a program of genetic engineering whereby they would accelerate the physical and intellectual development of certain of the bipedal creatures.

Exceedingly patient, detached, almost emotionless in its approach to scientific projects, the reptilian race experimented with skin pigmentation, facial and body hair, height, weight, and intelligence in their efforts to improve developing humankind.

At the same time, of course, the natural process of selection and survival was taking place on the planet, so that by the time

the serpentine scientists had created cities of rather sophisticated inhabitants about 200,000 years ago, Neanderthal man
was just beginning to huddle together in caves.

By 100,000 years ago, the genetic engineers from beyond
the stars looked with pride upon a flourishing culture that spread
its influence throughout every section of the planet. These
extraterrestrially accelerated people, known today as the inhabitants of the legendary Atlantis, Lemuria, and Mu, structured a technology which sought to replicate that of the Serpent
Gods from the stars. They also learned how to manipulate and
to control the natural energies of Earth.

Regretfully, however, the majority of these forces and technologies were developed for purposes of exploitation and destruction, inspired by a spirit of fierce competition among certain
factions within the Serpent Gods themselves. Tragically, little
thought had been given by the reptilian engineers to teaching
humankind about the individual sovereignty of others or about
the hardships that one's acts of self-aggrandizement might cause
another.

And to complicate matters, the humans had turned out to be
a prolific species, which seemed to take delight in repro-
ducing. What had begun as an earthly paradise had been slowly
transformed into land of civil strife and internal warrings.

A great catastrophe is said to have submerged the great
island kingdoms beneath the oceans. Nearly all the Atlanteans
and Lemurians were drowned, with the exception of the mer-
chant marine and those who managed to escape in boats or
rafts. The survivors of the disaster spread the story of the death
of a world before our own from east to west, and the tale has
been passed to our own time via the many variations of the
Great Deluge legends.

What is discomforting to consider in this hypothesis is that
the reptilian engineers may have been the ones responsible for
the great cataclysms that submerged an experiment that got out
of hand. They may well have come to the conclusion that they
had been wrong in interfering with the evolutionary process of
Earth. A decision may have been reached to "correct" their
error and henceforth to pass an edict that their kind can never
again interact with us.

Old traditions speak of a war between the forces of light
and darkness which raged in humankind's prehistory. Whether
such a conflict occurred in the destruction of that world before

our own that we remember in our species' collective unconscious as Atlantis or whether the struggle took place between
rival extraterrestrial forces, there exists awesome evidence that
someone was exercising power of formidable energy.

According to some traditions, the Sons of the Light van-
quished certain Black Magicians who sought to enslave developing humankind, and wherever the disciples of chaos had
built fortifications of earthly power, "the smoke rose up like
that from a mighty furnace."

There are accounts of sand melted into glass in certain desert
areas, of hill forts with vitrified portions of stone walls, of the
remains of ancient cities that had been destroyed by what appeared to have been extreme heat—far beyond that which could
have been scorched by the torches of primitive armies. In each
instance, the trained and experienced archaeologists who encountered such anomalous finds have stressed the point that
none of these catastrophes had been caused by volcanoes, by
lightning, by crashing comets, or by conflagrations set by humankind.

Albion W. Hart, one of the first engineers to graduate from
Massachusetts Institute of Technology, was assigned a project
in the interior of Africa. While he and his men were traveling
to an almost inaccessible region, they had first to cross a great
expanse of desert. At the time, he was puzzled and quite unable
to explain a large area of greenish glass which covered the
sands as far as he could see.

"Later on during his life," wrote Margarethe Casson in *Rocks
and Minerals* (No. 396, 1972), "he passed by the White Sands
area after the first atomic explosion there, and he recognized
the same type of silica fusion which he had seen fifty years
earlier in the African desert."

In western Arabia there are twenty-eight fields of blackened
and shattered stones that cover as many as 7000 miles each.
The stones are densely grouped, as if they might be the remains
of cities, sharp-edged, and burned black. Experts have decreed
that they are not volcanic in origin, but appear to date from
the period when Arabia was thought to be a lush and fruitful
land.

In 1947, in the Euphrates valley of southern Iraq, where
certain traditions place the Garden of Eden, where the ancient
inhabitants of Sumer encountered the man-god Ea, exploratory
digging unearthed a layer of fused, green glass. Archaeologists

could not restrain themselves from noting the resemblance that the several-thousand-year-old fused glass bore to the desert floor at White Sands, New Mexico, after the first nuclear blasts in modern times had melted sand and rock.

A similar discovery has been made at the site of Catal Hüyük in north-central Turkey, thought to be one of he oldest cities in the world. According to archaeological evidence, the city appeared to have been fully civilized and then, suddenly, to have died out.

Archaeologists were astonished to find thick layers of burned brick at one of the levels, called VIa. The blocks had been fused together by such intense heat that the effects had penetrated to a depth more than a meter below the level of the floors, where it carbonized the earth, the skeletal remains of the dead, and the burial gifts that had been interred with them. All bacterial decay had been halted by the tremendous heat.

When a large ziggurat in Babylonia was excavated, it presented the appearance of having been struck by a terrible fire that had split it down to its foundation. In other parts of the ruins, large sections of brickwork had been scorched into a vitrified state. Several masses of brickwork had been rendered into a completely molten state. Even large boulders found near the ruins had been vitrified.

The royal buildings at the north Syrian site known as Alalakh had been so completely burned that the very core of the thick walls were filled with bright red, crumbling mud-bricks. The mud and lime wall plaster had been vitrified, and basalt wall slabs had, in some areas, actually melted.

Between India's Ganges River and the Rajmahal Hills are scorched ruins which contain large masses of stone that have been fused and hollowed. Certain travelers who have ventured to the heart of the Indian forests have reported ruins of cities in which the walls have become huge slabs of crystal, due to some intense heat.

In the United States, the Mohave Desert has large circular or polygonal areas that are coated with a hard substance very much like opaque glass.

While exploring Death Valley in 1850, William Walker claimed to have come upon the ruins of an ancient city. An end of the large building within the rubble had had its stones melted and vitrified.

Walker went on to state that the entire region between the

Gila and St. John rivers was spotted with ruins. In each of the ancient settlements he had found evidence that they had been burned out by fire intense enough to have liquified rock. Paving blocks and stone houses had been split with huge cracks, as if seared by some gigantic cleaver of fire.

The ruins of the Seven Cities, located near the equator in the Province of Piaui, Brazil, appear to be the scene of a monstrous chaos. Since no geological explanation has yet been construed to fit the evidence before the archaeologists, certain of those who have investigated the site have said that the manner in which the stones have been dried out, destroyed, and melted provokes images of Sodom and Gomorrah.

Until the radiocarbon dating method was developed in the late 1940s, it was often a matter of argument when it came to arriving at the exact date of an archaeological site. The consensus of academic opinion most often placed the Amerindian's ancestors on this continent at not more than 3000 years ago, and if the dig produced artifacts that seemed the slightest bit controversial, the experts simply fell back on their favorite theories and prejudices and denounced their opponents.

Some archaeologists, of course, did accept the physical evidence of the spearhead between a *Bison antiquus'* ribs as testimony that man had been near what is now Folsom, New Mexico, over 10,000 years ago. Many of the most skeptical conceded that the spear points found amidst the bones of extinct horses, camels, and mammoths in a dig near Clovis, New Mexico, in 1932, proved that human hunters had stalked the great beasts more than 12,000 years ago.

But in spite of the dozens of finds during the 1930s which uncovered Paleo-Indian artifacts *in situ* with the bones of extinct elephants and bison, the most *avant-garde* of the archaeologists would only place humans upon the continent around 10,000 years ago, while the conservative still argued adamantly for a more recent arrival of 3000 years.

A human skull, mandible, and ribs, which had been found at the base of a sea cliff at Del Mar, California, in 1929, and conventionally catalogued, was, in 1974, dated to 48,000 years ago by Dr. Jeffrey Bada, a chemist at the Skipps Institute. Since that time, Bada has dated human skeletal remains at four other California sites as being 27,000, 39,000, 45,000 and 70,000 years in age.

In recent years, conservative archaeologists have had their

world turned inside out, but only the most open-minded of scientists would dare to read a complete dossier of the remarkable and provocative discoveries concerning early humans in North America.

There is, for example, the data concerning the 1898 find of H. Flagler Cowden and his brother, Charles, who unearthed the fossil remains of a giant female, over seven feet tall, who they speculated was a member of a race of large primitives who had vanished from the face of the earth some 100,000 years ago.

Astonishingly, the Cowdens had found their giant woman in Death Valley, an area that, while desolate in modern times, may have been an inlet for the Pacific Ocean in prehistoric times. In the same strata with the female skeleton were the remains of extinct camels, elephants, palm trees, towering ferns, and fish life.

It is quite likely that the Cowdens' estimate of 100,000 years ago may be excessive, even though the brothers had based their conclusion on the amount of silica in the soil and the sands and by the state of petrification of the skeletal remains, along with the crystallization and opalization of the bone marrow. Perhaps, we may reason, 50,000 years would be adequate—and almost as heretical.

One thing is certain: If the giant female was seven feet, six inches tall, then, assuming the same kind of height ratio which exists in modern times, the males of the vanished valley paradise would have been eight feet tall. Neither Neanderthal nor Cro-Magnon were taller than *Homo sapiens sapiens*; and the Shoshones, Paiutes, Cosos and other desert tribes who had occupied the valley at the time of the European invasion of the continent were no taller than the invaders. Who can identify these mysterious giants of Death Valley?

It is difficult not to feel tiny prickles of recognition of genetic engineering when our further reading informs us that the Cowdens discovered a number of anomalous physical appendages and attributes not found in contemporary man. They noted a number of several extra "buttons" at the base of a woman's spine, "and every indication betraying the woman and her people as endowed with tail-like appendages." The brothers also found that the woman had canine teeth twice the size and length of modern man.

[The hasty will scoff at the suggestion that giant humans

with tails once walked the Americas, but the *New England Journal of Medicine* of May 20, 1982, described the birth of a baby with a two-inch-long tail. The slender, tapered growth was surgically removed at Children's Hospital Medical Center in Boston. Dr. Fred D. Ledley saw the appendage as a "vivid example of man's place in evolution."

While noting that few tail cases have been documented in the latter part of this century, Dr. Ledley stated that the "well-formed caudal appendage" represented a "striking clinical confrontation with the reality of evolution."

Humans may have diverted from their most closely related tail-bearing primates twenty-five million years ago, Dr. Ledley agreed, but "human genes still contain information for tail formation."]

Then there is the account of the party of miners working near Bridalveil Falls, California, who, in July 1895, found the tomb of a woman whose skeletal remains were six feet, eight inches in length. The miners had found the Amazon behind a wall of rock that had been shaped and fitted together with an apparent knowledge of masonry. When they had broken through the wall, they hoped that they had stumbled upon some ancient treasure trove.

Instead of riches, however, the men found that they had blundered into the burial chamber of a very large woman. The corpse had been wrapped in animal skins and covered with a fine gray powder. She was clutching a child to her breast.

Scientists in Los Angeles agreed that the mummy was that of a woman from a race that had flourished on the continent long before the Amerindian had become dominant. Their consensus was that she would have stood over seven feet tall in life, thereby making the males of her kind at least eight feet tall.

A newspaper account dated April 4, 1874, tells of a veritable catacomb of giantlike skeletal remains that was unearthed when workmen were opening a way for the railroad between Wildon and Garrysburg, North Carolina:

The skulls were nearly an inch in thickness; the teeth were filed sharp . . . the enamel perfectly preserved; the bones were of wonderful strength, the femur being as long as the leg of an ordinary man, the stature of the body being probably as great as eight or nine feet. . . . The

bodies were found closely packed together, laid tier on
tier. . . . The mystery is, who these were, to what race
they belonged, to what era, and how they came to be
buried there. . . .

An article in the *New York Times* for May 4, 1912, gives
us another clue in our bizarre mystery story. Eighteen skeletons
were found while excavating a mound near Lake Delavan,
Wisconsin. The remains of the males were those of giants, with
remarkably large heads, while the women were of normal size
with smaller heads.

Subsequent news articles of the find described the males as
possessed of sloping foreheads with nasal bones that protruded
far above the cheekbones. "Their jawbones were long and
pointed, bearing a minute resemblance to the head of a monkey.
The teeth in front of the jaw are regular molars."

The *New York Times* index proves a good reference re-
source. On December 2, 1930, a newspaper carried an item
about a similar find near a mining town, Sayopa, Sonora, 300
miles south of the Mexican border. A mining engineer, J.E.
Coker, reported finding "bodies of men, averaging eight feet
in height . . . buried tier by tier."

On February 14, 1936, the *Times* ran a piece datelined
Managua, Nicaragua, which told of the skeleton of a gigantic
man, *sans* skull, that had been unearthed in the Chontales
district near the Mico River: "The ribs are a yard long and four
inches wide and the shin bone is too heavy for one man to
carry. 'Chontales' is an Indian word, meaning 'wild man'. . . ."

On June 9, 1936, an article with a Miami, Florida, dateline
told of human skeletons eight feet long imbedded in the sand
of an uninhabited little island off the southern part of the state.
Three fishermen had brought home a piece of a skull to prove
their story:

> E.M. Miller, zoologist at the University of Miami, said
> the mandible was that of a man and was probably several
> hundred years old. . . . "It is entirely probable that this
> find might be important," he commented. The men said
> that the skulls were unusually thick, the jaws protruded,
> and the eye sockets were high in the head.

Whether or not the data cited in this chapter merits comfortable consideration or whether you wish to place it on "hold,"

there seems to be a growing amount of evidence—a bit more than circumstantial—which suggests that an organized program of genetic engineering was conducted on Earth by agents of an extraterrestrial civilization of advanced technology. Judging from certain prior discoveries which have been made on this continent, it would seem that North America in particular may have served as a vast and unique laboratory for a number of experimental programs.

The question of what it is to be human may begin to acquire new, dramatic, and startling answers. And the specific question of *how* humankind evolved on the North American continent suggests answers that may be considered too startling and iconoclastic for the anthropological traditionalist.

We may continue to acquire entry after entry in our journal of anomalous skeletal remains:

*Tioga Point, Bradford County, Pennsylvania* . . . the bones of 68 men . . . average height, seven feet.

*Dresbach, Minnesota* . . . the bones of men over eight feet tall . . . discovered in huge earthworks.

*LaCrescent, Minnesota* . . . large metal skillets, together with bones of men of huge stature.

*Ellisburg, Pennsylvania* . . . skeleton of a man close to eight feet in length.

And what of the legends of the Allegewi?

The oral traditions of the Delaware and the Sioux Indians tell of a race of "great stature, but cowardly" with whom they entered into conflict. The Allegheny River and Mountains are named after the Allegewi, but the Iroquois Confederacy drove the giants out of their strong, walled cities, and the Sioux finished them off when they attempted to relocate in what is now Minnesota.

Has our species been genetically engineered?

Was early *Homo sapiens* guided around some evolutionary dead ends?

Only the human species, among species in the natural state, comes in such a great diversity of "breeds." It is as if we have been domesticated and controlled in a manner similar to the ways that we employed to assist Nature in creating the great varieties of domesticated dogs and cats. In any other of the primate species, such as the gorilla, all of the members are essentially alike.

If one were to make an extensive study of the characteristics peculiar to each genus of the primates, *Homo* has three hundred and twelve differences from his closest cousins among all the creatures on the planet. To itemize only a few, we may note humankind's dexterity with thumb and index finger; the big buttocks for walking; the thick layer of subcutaneous fat beneath the outer skin; the mobile facial muscles, capable of over one hundred subtle expressions; the furless skin.

Of greater importance is the explosive speed at which the neocortex of *Homo sapiens* has evolved in the last 500,000 years. If all the primates began the evolutionary trek three to five million years ago, why was it that only humankind has become so clearly dominant and superior?

The brain of the human is three times the size of the gorilla. It has ten billion neurons, ten times as many as the chimpanzees. Human intelligence is one hundred times greater than that of any ape, since intellect leaps geometrically with increased neurons.

And why is it that today the intelligence of apes remains static, never making any dramatic leaps forward, never accomplishing any breakthroughs? In spite of numerous experiments being conducted, it seems doubtful that extensive training has been able to improve a chimpanzee's intelligence quotient.

The consensus among modern anthropologists and paleontologists is that evolution is a very slow and uniform process and that no animal species, other than *Homo sapiens*, has shown any dramatic or sudden evolutionary changes within the last few million years. Any major change in an animal's size, limbs, internal organs, or basic structure takes tens of millions of years, according to the experts who examine the fossil bones of various species. Humankind itself, so states the general agreement among scholars, did not change qualitatively for about 900,000 years; but then, only about 15,000 years ago, *Homo sapiens'* brain suddenly expanded to the point where he could begin to fashion civilizations.

Is it too heretical to suggest that humankind may have received some external assistance in its evolutionary trek?

Does it remove humankind too much from the center of the universe to wonder if there might not have been a world of experimental and developmental humans before our own?

The world that permits you to read this book, watch television, drive an automobile, and ride in an airplane is said to have begun in Sumer six thousand years ago when a dying star's flaring brilliance caught the attention of a primitive neo-lithic humankind and made them receptive to the advent of cultural stirrings. Almost "overnight" the ancient inhabitants of this region were able to fashion a civilization of cities, agriculture, law, and the arts.

But could there not have been a world *before* our own? A very strange world of genetic engineering which existed for thousands of years before ours began?

Why is it that only human females have pain during child-birth? Why was our mother Eve cursed with travail?

Was it because she ate the apple in Paradise?

Or was it because she received the serpent's child in the wonderful, magical gardens of the extraterrestrial's laborato-ries?

Dr. Paul MacLean, one of the world's most eminent brain researchers, theorizes that during the course of evolution hu-mans have acquired three very different brains: a primal mind from reptiles, an emotional mind from early mammals, and a rational mind from more recent mammals. The very center of our brain is composed of the primitive reptilian brain, largely responsible for our self-preservation.

Dr. Carl Sagan made extensive use of Dr. MacLean's the-ories in his best-selling book, *The Dragons of Eden*; and the triune brain hypothesis has stimulated numerous scholars in the social sciences. Is it really too much to suggest that there may be an even more dramatic, more *direct*, reason for our reptilian heritage?

In my more than twenty years of investigation into the UFO mystery, I have heard those human participants of close en-counters with alleged UFOnauts most often describe the aliens as smallish, reptilian-appearing humanoids with disproportion-ately large heads. Often, as I listened to these eyewitnesses recounting their experiences, my memory provided me with silent confirmation, for my own visitor on that long-ago Oc-tober night had a preternaturally large head for his size.

The Serpent People may have an extremely large brain ca-pacity, perhaps 3000 cc or even 4000 cc compared with hu-mankind's average of 1300 to 1500 cc. From what we can estimate of the primates, the subhumans, if you will, who were extant at the time of the reptilian species' interaction, they may have had a brain capacity of about 450 cc.

Even though the genetic engineers were no doubt cognizant

of the implications of sudden brain expansion, the leap in cranial size which they had prompted came in much too short a time for an accompanying evolutionary change in the female body to have occurred. Although things have moderated, the two mutations have still not completely meshed. Woman must still accommodate a too-big baby's head with a too-small internal organ and birth canal.

On September 8, 1981, biologist Dr. Thomas E. Wagner and his coworkers at Ohio University announced the first successful transfer of a gene from one animal species to another—from rabbits to mice and then to the mice's offspring.

If we now have begun the process of engineering the transfer of certain traits from one creature to another, we will soon be able to create genetically new animals or to transfer a particularly desired trait within the same species. We are so close to being able to accomplish with other creatures that which the Serpent People apparently did with developing humankind.

Quoting from a news story in the *Washington Post*:

In short, Wagner said, "We have demonstrated not only that we can introduce a gene into a species but that when the animal becomes mature, it not only contains the new genetic material but is making the desired product. And that its offspring are producing the same product, this new protein of rabbit origin.

A large part of the "trick" that makes this possible, he said, is injecting the foreign DNA into the egg cells at the right moment.

For the past eight years, he explained, he has worked on "the very early process of fertilization" from the male, or sperm, point of view—what happens to the sperm cell when it enters the egg.

What happens is that the sperm cell's head penetrates the egg wall, then quickly swells into what is called the pronucleus.

"This," Wagner said, "is the one time in an animal's entire life history when it is normal for it to accept foreign genetic material. It is a privileged time, a time when, by definition, the egg must be in a vulnerable state to allow the integration of foreign DNA.

"We're essentially tricking the egg into believing the

rabbit DNA is part of the male's DNA that it must accept anyway."

In 1979, about 17,000 bovine pregnancies were produced by superovulation and embryo transfer in North America alone. The major use of such techniques was to increase the productive rate of the more valuable cows.

Professor Edward J. Kollar of the University of Connecticut received the 1980–1981 Schour Memorial Science Award for making mice grow "bird" teeth:

> Kollar, an oral-biology professor, is convinced birds have the ability to grow teeth because fossils of ancient birds have reptilelike teeth.
>
> To activate the gene to grow teeth, Kollar grafted a five-day-old chick embryo's epithelium, which forms the outer enamel of the tooth, on to the molar buds of mouse embryos and implanted the graft in laboratory mice. The result was whole teeth with an enamel layer provided by chicken cells. The teeth did not look like mouse teeth, but rather like the teeth found in bird fossils. (*United Press International*)

Our own science is within cosmic moments of achieving such feats of genetic engineering as might have been worked upon humankind in its prehistory.

In 1953, Francis Crick and James Watson launched a "biological revolution" with their discovery of DNA, the master molecule that contains the genetic code. In 1962, for their successful solution of the DNA puzzle, Crick and Watson shared the Nobel Prize for Physiology and Medicine with physicist Maurice Wilkins.

Today, Dr. Crick has boldly suggested that the seeds of life on Earth may have been sent here in a rocket launched from some faraway planet by "creatures like ourselves." Science writer David Rorvik explored such a provocative theory, together with other subjects, in an interview which appeared in the March 1982 issue of *Omni* magazine:

> At [a meeting in Soviet Armenia in 1971] we discussed the idea that uniformity of the genetic code makes it look

as if life went through a rather narrow bottleneck. In
addition, I came to realize that sufficient time had elapsed
for life to have evolved twice—that is, a civilization
capable of sending out rockets could already have come
into existence at the time the solar system and the earth
got going. Leslie Orgel [a biochemist at the Salk Insti-
tute] and I, in collaboration, came up with the idea of a
directed panspermia.

When asked by Rorvik to comment on precisely which things
made the theory of panspermia attractive to him, Dr. Crick
replied: "The easiest way to see that it's attractive is to realize
that we might find ourselves doing the same thing a thousand
or two thousand years from now, seeding life in the same way."

One of the greatest gulfs between humankind and the primates lies in the exploratory instinct. The apes live together in
bands, small pseudotribal units, never functioning as single
animals. Young apes are never allowed to roam or to explore
beyond the perimeters of their immediate environment. Nor
does the limited brain of the ape ever permit the creature,
whether young or old, to explore any areas of thought beyond
those of eating, mating, and self-protection.

The human child, on the other hand, begins to explore the
day it begins to crawl. All through childhood there is a drive
to seek out the new and the unknown. No other species of
animal even remotely displays the insatiable and driving curiosity of *Homo*.

The quantum leap from restricted, nonexploratory primate
to space-trekking human in a brief million years could well
have been due to the catalyst of genetic engineering at the
hands of the Serpent People. The restless and eternal drive to
learn everything and to travel everywhere may have been in-
stilled into our DNA construct by intelligences who had already
begun to chart the universe.

The reptilian humanoids came to this planet and viewed it
as a great biological laboratory. They must have seen a hundred
thousand possibilities for this terrestrial ball. They must also
have computed that it would take the slow process of evolution
a hundred million years to alter a species or to develop a new
one. For whatever specific reason they chose to become in-

volved, they made the decision to accelerate evolution and to fashion a rational creature before its time.

It is obvious that the Serpent People did not always get the results that they wanted. Remember the findings of those excavators who discovered fossils and skeletal remains of primitive men and women over seven feet tall; hominids with horns; giants with double rows of teeth; prehistoric peoples with sharply slanting foreheads and fanged jaws; pygmy cultures which had survived in living form with primitive awareness. Such anomalous discoveries might cause us to consider that even the monster-humans of mythology might have been abortive genetic experiments which were rejected by the Serpent People as they sought to achieve *Homo sapiens*.

Now, obviously, I am taking advantage of an author's prerogative and supposing a great deal in my hypothesis of the intervention of a reptilian species with humankind's planetary evolution. Regardless of how many facts I may have gathered for the reader's assessment, the bulk of my data is, admittedly, based on largely intuitive tinglings in my own brain.

But, remember, I admitted at the outset that I believe that the scene with which I opened this chapter would one day occur in reality. And I also believe that one day such alien interaction with humankind in its prehistory will be firmly established as undeniable fact.

Years ago, when I was actively engaged in UFO research, I realized how presumptuous it would be for any human being to attempt to categorize any alien in an extensive manner. How could we even begin to guess what interested them philosophically, what stimulated their senses, what stirred them emotionally? Perhaps none of the concepts that I have just named would have any real meaning to them.

Yet, if you assume with me that such a reptilian species— or any alien species—does, in fact, exist on *some* planet in *some* galaxy, then it is difficult not to envision them rising in the morning and looking up at the sun. It is impossible not to assume that they eat a breakfast, go to work, curse traffic, make love with their mates, and spoil their children.

We assume these things because we human beings do these kinds of things, and it seems that we must anthropomorphize everything which we attempt to understand. It is disturbing to those of us who are convinced such aliens do exist to consider that we may have few subjects of comparison with them.

We feel a moment of panic when such a realization grips us. How, after all, can we ever hope to understand them if we don't know their favorite foods, their special preferences for environmental surroundings, and what kind of music they like best for listening or dancing?

On occasion, I have fantasized about a group of Neanderthals who stumble through a time warp and come upon a modern suburban home.

About the only things of which they would be able to make any kind of sense would be the baseball bats and the golf clubs. They would assume that the sticks were some kind of swinging and striking instruments.

The furniture in the house would probably have little meaning to them, to say nothing of the electronic utilities. A clock on the wall would be incomprehensible, since they would have no concept of time and numbers.

At this point in our intellectual and scientific evolution, we might be little more than Neanderthals in comparison to the reptilian aliens. And that may be defensive thinking. We may not be *that* far along in comparison with their technology. It might be extremely difficult for our twentieth century technologists to measure up with entities who may have a different perspective to every entry in the cosmic encyclopedia.

In my opinion, then, it was a reptilian extraterrestrial species that lifted developing humankind out of the primeval muck and engineered the species into thinking nonanimals. But, then, with what appears to be a peculiar kind of detachment that characterizes their own kind, they left their various hybrid remnants in the rubble of crumbling civilizations and soared off to practice a future policy of nonintervention.

It was left to the multidimensional, spiritual beings, whom we refer to as the Star Gods, to bring the hybrid peoples together and to give each of them an awareness of the divine seed, the Soul, that lies within the fleshly body structure.

# Chapter Six

*⌇*

# THE LEGACY OF THE STAR GODS

> In considering the future of religion, it is appropriate to ask
> what the unknown might yield in the next few decades that
> would have relevance to man's view of his relationship to
> the cosmos. A major event . . . would be the discovery of
> extraterrestrial life wherein we would become members of
> a community of life, participants in a drama bigger than we
> could have dreamed.
>
> *Theodore J. Gordon*

Sir John Eccles, winner of the Nobel Prize for medicine in
1963, is the complete scientist, philosopher, metaphysician.
As the scientist who demonstrated the transmission of electrical
impulses in the brain, he probably knows more about the workings of humankind's mental machinery than anyone in known
history.

Sir John has declared that his research has led him to con-
clude that evolution alone cannot explain man's awareness of
himself. Sir John has become increasingly convinced that there
must have been the intervention of some transcendental agency
in the infusion into humankind of Soul. Simply stated, he

maintains that the brain and the mind are separate entities which interact, but it is only the brain that is the product of genetic evolution.

In an interview with Sandy Rovner of the *Washington Post* (April, 1981), Sir John explained his hypothesis:

> I am an evolutionist, of course, but I don't believe that evolution is the final story.... The genetic code and natural selection explain quite a lot, but evolution doesn't explain how I came to exist. It doesn't explain even the origin of consciousness.... If you look at the most modern texts on evolution, you find nothing about mind and consciousness. They assume that it just comes automatically with the development of the brain. But that's not an answer. If my uniqueness of self is tied to the genetic uniqueness of self that built my brain, the odds against myself existing are 10 to the 10-thousandth against.
>
> It is just too improbable to wait around to get the right constructed brain for you. The brain is a computer, you see. Each of us has a computer and we are the programmers of this computer. [We were] born . . . with what this wonderful structure of evolution and genetic coding have wrought.... But the soul is this unique creation that is ours for life. It is us. We are experiencing, remembering, creating, suffering, imagining. All of this is processed here with the soul central to it.

I am not suggesting that Sir John Eccles would agree with my hypothesis, but I cite the above as a kind of oblique support that an extraterrestrial group of genetic engineers could have involved themselves in the hybridization and the acceleration of at least a segment of our species. The body and brain of which we are so proud may have been largely crafted by an external source through a process of deliberate genetic programming. But then, perhaps many thousands of years later, the remnant of that extraterrestrial experimentation blended with a higher intelligence, who produced pockets of gifted progeny whenever their spiritual seed fell upon fertile ground.

The earliest civilization of which science has any records flowered among the Sumerians of ancient Mesopotamia. A quantum leap in humankind's intellectual development occurred in Sumer 6000 years ago when cuneiform writing was

invented to record a dramatic starburst. Every pulsating thrust
of the technology with which humankind surrounds itself today
was initiated when a star died in a dramatic, brilliant explosion.

The psychological and cultural impact of the supernova on
the inhabitants of Sumer was overwhelming. Literally "overnight" in evolutionary terms, the Sumerians gave the world a
law code, the first love song, the first school system, the first
parliament, and the first directory of pharmaceutical concoc-
tions. The origins of contemporary Western culture were nursed
in Sumer, the cradle of civilization. The roots of the Judeo-
Christian religious beliefs grew from the "tree of knowledge,"
the Garden of Eden, which tradition places in that same area.

Astronomers recognize the nearest and brightest supernova
ever witnessed by humankind as Vela X, now a faintly flashing
pulsar about 1300 light-years from our solar system. George
Michanowsky, a specialist in Mesopotamian astronomy, saw
how the very first and most fundamental symbol of Sumerian
script was one which represented "star." He went on to show
how the first word ever written by a human soon became linked
with the symbol for "deity," thus communicating "star god."
Michanowsky saw the death-blaze of Vela X to have been such
a profound sky show that it became a "cultural organizing
principle" that forced human knowledge to take a dramatic leap
forward.

But was there something more that took place at that time?

The priest-historian Berossus chronicled the account of
Oannes, half-man, half-fish, who surfaced from the Persian
Gulf to instruct the early inhabitants of Mesopotamia in the
arts of civilization. Oannes was said to be one who was possessed of an insight into letters, sciences, and every kind of
art. Oannes was but an ancient Greek form of Ea, the star god
of the Sumerians.

Were the Sumerians so overwhelmingly inspired by the starburst that they were stimulated into creating writing, law, ed-
ucation, and many of the essential concepts of the modern
science?

Or had they received some overt physical assistance and
instruction from survivors who might have been escaping the
supernova, the death of their sun?

Reference to a god who was said to be half-man, half-fish
suggests, once again, an amphibious intelligence. However,
we may recall a later Son of God, a "fisher of men," whose

followers identified themselves to one another by making the sign of a fish.

The great metaphysician Rudolf Steiner theorized that the people of our prehistory (the Atlanteans) had been largely guided and directed by a higher order of beings who interacted and communicated with certain humans—the smartest, the strongest, the most intellectually flexible. Eventually, these select humans produced what might be called demigods, divine human beings, who, in turn, could relay instructions from higher intelligences.

In effect, Steiner may have given us another definition of the progeny that the ancient Hebrews named "Nephilim," which does, in fact, mean demigod, men of "great renown."

Steiner went on to speculate that within the larger evolving human race were the descendents of those divine-human hybrid beings, men and women who are animated by higher ideals, who regard themselves as children of a divine, universal power. It need not be overemphasized that the larger body of humankind is devoted to the service of egotism, materialism, and selfish, personal interests.

Steiner believed that within what he termed the emerging "Sixth Post-Atlantean Race" would be children of the divine universal power who would be able to initiate those men and women who have developed their faculty of thought so that they might better unite themselves with the divine. The children of the divine universal power, those who have the "seed" within them, will be able to initiate the more advanced members of humankind. People so initiated will be able to receive revelations and perform what others will consider miracles. The initiates will go on to become the mediators between humankind and the higher intelligences.

The whole point of the efforts of these higher intelligences is to enable humankind to become more independent, more able to stand on its own feet without having to rely on the higher order of beings that directed us in ancient times.

Francie has been told that there is a gathering of the Seed, a coming together of these so-called children of the divine going on right now.

She does not seem to be alone in this belief. Many others have written to share with us their understanding that such an awakening, such a gathering, will begin during this time in which we now live, the time of Steiner's emerging Sixth Root Race.

In a remarkable series of channeling sessions with Francie, the multidimensional being, Kihief, who has communicated with her since she was a child of five, relayed the following account of the Star Gods' visitation to Earth:

The Star Gods were inhabitants of a planet that had been in the process of a vibrational transition from matter to energy. About 12,000 years ago, shortly before their Sun was about to become a supernova, certain of their kind chose to leave their planet on a mission to seek out a cousin species to whom they might bequeath their concepts of spirituality, of morality, of aesthetic appreciation of the fruits of the Source, and their penchant for structure and self-discipline.

When they discovered Earth on their quest for heirs, they found a place of chaos. On the one hand they encountered the remnants of a civilization which the reptilian species had cultivated and had accelerated in clear violation of the galactic laws of noninterference with the natural evolutionary processes of any planet. On the other, they found a primitive, but vitally emerging, *Homo sapiens*, who were beginning to establish the rudiments of culture in certain pockets scattered about the globe.

Since the Serpent People had elected to accelerate the natural evolutionary pace of humankind and had, in essence, created beings without soul-knowledge, the Star Gods felt that they had no choice other than to interact with both the developing primitives and the members of the advanced *Homo* cultures and to provide them with the spiritual seeding that the more material and detached reptilian extraterrestrials had little interest in providing.

The Bible's references to God's anger at the serpent's interference with the natural flow of things in the Garden of Eden may have been the ancient people's understanding of the Star Gods' disgust with the reptilian genetic engineers' failure to instill spiritual teachings along with material knowledge. The Star Gods may have believed the reptilians to have been very wrong to have interfered with the natural evolutionary processes on this planet. Perhaps they understood that, to the reptilian people, developing humankind was nothing more than a scientific project. *Homo sapiens* was merely a laboratory animal with promise and potential—a creature with a future that they sought to make better.

But there was no way that the Serpent People could create a Soul in a laboratory. It was left to the Star Gods to teach humankind of the things of the spirit. It was left to them to complete humankind's creation.

Those from the dying star had little difficulty in converting the Atlantean priestcraft to their spiritual concepts. Since the Star Gods, as well as their star and planetary system, were rapidly raising in frequency in a return to pure energy, it was a simple matter for them to manifest as supernatural beings, able to appear and disappear, able to walk through walls, able to travel from one distant point to another in the twinkling of an eye.

For those more primitive humans, developing according to natural process, the Star Gods truly appeared to be angels and godlike entities. Later, when the greatness of Atlantis had passed to legends and memories, the Star Gods guided its survivors to areas where they might best keep the smoldering flame of civilization aglow.

By the time that Vela X illuminated the sky with its brilliance, the intergalactic missionaries were ready. When, six thousand years ago, the starburst captured the attention of humankind all over the world, the Star Gods took advantage of the diversionary action to enter settlement after settlement with the teachings of law, agriculture, unconditional love, art, music, moral concerns, communal responsibility—and most importantly, the awareness of the facet of the Divine Essence that manifests within each human being.

On occasion, the Star Gods materialized in full physical expression to walk among the inhabitants of the cities of Sumer and Egypt. Most often, however, they utilized the priestcraft and exceptional humans of the natural process to serve as their three-dimensional representatives. The Star Gods were often instrumental in accomplishing a genetic engineering of their own when they would encourage the mating of men and women of high abilities, culled from the emerging primitives and the descendents of the reptilian experiment.

It was to the Star God's children by proxy that they bequeathed programmed crystals of knowledge and enlightenment and crystals of energy. It was such crystals, according to certain occult traditions, that powered Noah's ark and provided the energy by which direct communication with the Star Gods was accomplished with the Ark of the Covenant.

The first recorded UFO sighting in modern times, that of civilian pilot Kenneth Arnold near Mt. Ranier on June 24, 1947, fired the imagination of the entire world. And then, in the 1950s when our own terrestrial space program came into being, many serious-minded men and women began to think of prehistoric man having had a dramatic series of interactions with a kindred species from another world, UFOnauts, who would have seemed like deities, like "sons of God" to primitive humankind.

In one of my notebooks which I kept at the time, I recorded the following thoughts as I was writing a UFO book, *Strangers from the Skies*, in 1966:

Our planet could actually have harbored a colony of extraterrestrial immigrants. I continue to be fascinated by the passage about the Nephilim, the Hebrew term used to describe demigods, or men of great reknown, those who were said to be the offspring of the sons of God and the daughters of men.

Interestingly, the word used to denote true giants, as far as great stature was concerned, was *rephaim*. The Israelites found such giants among the Canaanite inhabitants of Palestine. Among these *rephaim* were the Anakims of Philisa, the Emims of Moabs. Goliath was a Gittite, a man of great stature and bulk, but not a Nephilim.

I think it possible that the Nephilim were of greater height than their fellows, due to their ancestry; but, truly, I have come now to think of them as spiritual and intellectual, rather than physical, giants. I also consider it quite likely that they were programmed, so to speak, to aid their Earth brothers and sisters in collective mental, moral, ethical, and spiritual advancement of the species.

Who were their progenitors, the so-called sons of God?

It seems clear that the ancient Israelites thought them god-beings or angels, possessed of supernatural powers. I believe they came from another world, not a heaven, but an actual physical place. Where that was, whether a planet in our solar system or elsewhere, seems wasteful of energy to pursue. And, for all I know, they may well be still checking in on us from time to time, as witness the continued reports of UFOs.

I am struck by the remarkable diversity of the skeletal remains of humanoids that have been found on this continent. There have been discoveries of giants with double rows of teeth, sharply sloping foreheads, pointed jaws, extra vertebrae, unusually thick skulls, and, in one instance, with two-inch horns protruding from otherwise perfectly formed foreheads.

At the same time, it appears that there have been "wee people" thriving on this continent, virtual colonies of midgets.

*Harper's Magazine*, July 1869, tells of several burying grounds in Tennessee for tiny men and women, the tallest of whom was nineteen inches tall. They were all buried in stone coffins, their heads to the east, their hands folded across their chests. In the bend of the left arm of each skeleton lay a pint vessel made of ground stone or shell of a grayish color. The skeletons were all strong and well set, and their basic structures were well formed.

I wonder now, especially in reviewing the above, if this continent might not have served as some vast living laboratory in genetic engineering? Perhaps all these apparent stops and starts and deadened spurts of the *Homo sapiens* Family Tree might actually have been the failures and near-successes of ancient extraterrestrial scientists, whomever they might have been.

According to information received by Francie, the Star Gods continued to raise the vibrational frequency of their physical shells until they came to exist in a realm of intelligent energy where they began to function as Light Beings. On occasion, they lowered their vibratory frequencies in order to interact with sensitive humans—more frequently and more easily with those who bore within them the spiritual seed—so that they might relay teachings and guidance. The Light Beings could not remain in such contact for very long, however, or they would risk entrapment in the electromagnetic gravity field of Earth's dense matter.

"You remember segments of the Starseeded heritage, Brad," Francie said to me shortly after we had begun to work together in 1975. "You remember many things, for you have the seed within you.

"You know that you bear within you the truth of humankind's spiritual ancestry. You are descended from those men and women who were brought together by the Star Gods. So am I such a descendent. So are thousands and thousands of men and women who are being activated right now by memories bursting within them. It is as if genetic time-release capsules are exploding inside them and alerting them with the true knowledge of who they really are and what their mission on earth really is.

"The Serpent Person visited you when you were a child to see if their genetic experiment was blending with the implantation of the Star Gods' spiritual seed," Francie said, clutching at my hand. "That is all they can do now. Their council prohibits further interaction. But the experience *did* activate you. It did expand your awareness beyond this planet. All Star People are lightbearers, and we are to shine a light so that others may see their own path to the Source."

Francie went on to explain that we are not *physically* alien to this planet, but we have the spiritual seed within us. "It is your mission, Brad, to spread the knowledge of that seed throughout the entire Earth, so that all men and women will have the opportunity to achieve total awareness."

I told Francie that I was aware of the fact that I was not alone in such a mission. I acknowledged that there were many who spoke of enlightenment through total awareness of one's true potentials.

Francie's eyes became very serious. "But never omit one important element in your teaching of awareness. Never exclude the God-energy. The energies of Earth are magnificent, but they become elevated above the material plane only when they are linked with the energy from the Source which exists outside of this dimension."

In Rudolf Steiner's *Tenth Lecture on the Gospel of St. Luke*, he reflects that just as a plant cannot unfold its blossom immediately after the seed has been sown, so has humankind had to progress from stage to stage until the right knowledge could be brought to maturity at the right time.

Such spiritual prophets as Steiner have foretold that humankind is now entering the "fullness" of time when the Christ principle, cosmic consciousness, can once again become manifest. Sensitive observers of the contemporary scene have taken careful note of the fact that thousands of men and women throughout the world are being activated by a heightened state of awareness that many term "Christ consciousness." Each of these people is feeling the seed bringing forth new life within him or her and is concerned about the spiritual needs of the human souls around them.

Christ consciousness is a transformative energy which transcends orthodox Christianity. The Master Jesus became "Christed" and thereby presented us with an example of what it means to achieve a complete activation of the seed within us. Consider Steiner's words:

> The rest of humanity must now, in imitation of Christ, gradually develop what was present for thirty-three years on the Earth in the one single personality. It was only the impulse, as it were the seed, that Christ Jesus was able to implant into humanity at that time, and the seed must now unfold and grow ... The being who appeared on Earth as Christ had to take care that His message could be accessible to men immediately after his appearance, in a form that they could understand. He also had to make provision for individualities to appear later on and care for the spiritual needs of human souls. ...

To Steiner, the Christ energy is the catalyst that germinates the seed that great Spirit Beings implanted within their human offspring. There were, of course, the physical seeds of male and female, which intermingled to produce the whole human being. But there was also something in each human that did not arise from the blending of the two physical seeds. There was, so to speak, a "virgin birth," a something ineffable, Steiner says, which somehow flowed into the process of germination from quite a different source:

> Something unites with the seed of the human being that is not derived from father and mother, yet belongs to and is destined for him—something that is poured into his Ego and can be enabled through the Christ-principle. That in the human being which unites with the Christ-principle in the course of evolution is "virgin born"

and . . . is connected with the momentous transition accomplished at the time of Christ Jesus.

Spiritual history is replete with many sincere and insightful prophets and teachers who lived before the Master Jesus, but they could speak to their fellows only by using the faculties transmitted through their earthly natures. They used the energy and the wisdom of Earth.

Jesus, however, tapped into an awareness of that higher energy which comes from the realm of the Divine. He knew that a speck of this energy no larger than a mustard seed could exalt the human psyche. He knew that even the slightest infusion of this energy into the physical seed of male and female would transform the individual into a citizen of a higher dimension of reality, the "Kingdom of God." And, at the same time, he taught that the doorway to enter such a wondrous kingdom lay within the heart of each sincere pilgrim who sought to join him there.

"The *Christ Vibration* was patterned after the thought of the Creator," Francie observes in her book *Reflections from an Angel's Eye* (Berkley, 1982). "Within the constructs of this energy there exist the creative aspect and the guiding aspect, and those do interact with one another and create other systems of energy to exist, according to the pattern of the Divine Plan.

"The creative principle creates the patterns of the thoughts in accordance with the Divine Plan, as well as being the one that 'channels' the *creative* energies of God, which manifest as spiritual gifts from the Holy Ghost. It is this principle that also creates and forms the thoughts of all Universal Teachings that tell of the entire Plan of God. The spiritual gifts that it 'channels' from the creative aspect of God (the Holy Ghost) are those that will *reflect* God, making the Creator known to the world. . . ."

". . . Those who live according to the Divine Plan, regardless of religious affiliation, are *Christ children* . . . Jesus was an emissary of the *Christ Vibration* and was, therefore, a child of God, the son of God, an expression of the third sign of the trinity of Father, Mother, and Child.

"As *Children of the Christ Vibration*, we are to create harmonious energies—both physically and spiritually—as we interact with all the matter, both organic and inorganic. We are to cause patterned-energies to exist that will be in accordance with the Divine Plan, and we are to gather such energies to us so that upon our return to God we may bear gifts of the highest order. If our gifts vibrate with love, wisdom, and knowledge, then God will fulfill its desire to increase in complexity, to expand its energy, and to experience life in a myriad of forms and dimensions, thus accomplishing the Divine Plan."

"The importance of Jesus was not that he was a human like us," John W. White remarks, in the April 2, 1982 issue of *New Attitudes*, "but that we are gods like him—or at least we have the evolutionary potential to be."

White observes that while Jesus, the man, was a historical person, the "Christ" is an eternal, transpersonal condition of being. When we distinguish between the eternality of the "Christ consciousness" and the man Jesus, we can more completely understand the promise given in John 14:12: "Truly, truly, I say to you, he who believes in me will also do the work that I do; and greater works than these will he do...."

In White's view, Jesus was an evolutionary forerunner of the higher race that will inherit the earth, a "...race of people that will embody the Christ consciousness on a species-wide basis, rather than the sporadic individual basis seen earlier in history when an occasional avatar, such as Buddha or Jesus, appeared."

Jesus' knowledge of his true position was what led him to refer to himself most often as "the Son of Man," meaning the offspring of humanity, the New Adam who marked the beginning of still higher life-forms on earth.

White gives the name of *Homo Noeticus* (pertaining to higher consciousness) to the evolving form of humanity:

Because of their deepened awareness and self-understanding, the traditionally imposed forms, controls, and institutions of society are barriers to their full development. Their changed psychology is based on expression, not suppression, of feeling. Their motivation is cooperative and loving, not competitive and aggressive. Their sense of logic is multilevel, integrated, simultaneous; it is not linear, sequential, either-or. Their identity is sharing-collective, not isolated-individual. Their psychic abilities are used for benevolent and ethical purposes, not harmful and immoral ones. The conventional ways

of society do not satisfy them. The search for new ways
of living concerns them.

Jesus has shown us the way to the Kingdom of God, White
states, but it is up to the efforts of each individual to take
himself or herself there. The promise of Jesus was that all have
the capacity to grow to godlike stature, to evolve, to rise to a
higher state of being.

"For we are not simply human *beings*," White tells us, "we
are also human *becomings*, standing between two worlds, two
ages. . . . Each of us has the latent ability to take conscious
control of our evolution and thereby become members of the
New Age, the New Humanity . . . Jesus did not say that the
highest state of consciousness was his alone for all time. Rather,
he called us to follow him, from his example. He called us all
to share in a new condition, to be one in Christ, to be one in
the Christ consciousness which alone can dispel the darkness
of our lives and renew our very being . . . That state of consciousness is what Jesus exhibited and taught—cosmic consciousness, the Christ consciousness, the peace that passeth
understanding, the direct experience of divinity dwelling in us,
now and forever, creating us, preserving us, urging us on to
ever-higher states of being."

Numerous mystics and seers, quite apart from the Christian
tradition, have noted that there appears to have been some
dispensation of cosmic energy that occurred at the time when
the Master Jesus was seeking to raise awareness. Some believe
that when he preached about a new way that had come from
his Father's Kingdom and which had blended with the feminine
principle of the Holy Ghost, he was talking about a literal
transmission of energy being broadcast to Earth from some
higher realm.

Pentecost, those metaphysicians will say, was a powerful
demonstration of that energy. The apostles were so glowing
with the cosmic energy that they appeared to be on fire to those
who witnessed the absorption of the Christ principle into their
physical bodies.

It seems obvious to me that such an energy still exists here
on Earth. And it would appear to be rather easily demonstrable
that, in one way or another, humanity has not been the same
since the Christ Event.

Perhaps something truly was added to the energy of the

Earth Mother at that time—call it the Holy Spirit for lack of a better term—and hundreds of thousands of men and women are being activated by that same cosmic energy today. All over the planet, contemporary citizens of Earth are having their individual Pentecosts, as the seed within them, their spiritual legacy from beyond the stars, is being brought to fruition.

# Chapter Seven

## THE STAR PEOPLE: SEEDS AND HELPERS

Within the outer world of sense
Thought-power doth lose existence of its own;
The Spirit-worlds are finding
Once more their human offspring
Which must its seed discover
In spirit; but its fruit
In Self must ripen.

*Rudolf Steiner*

"Now is the time!" Francie and I declared in *The Star People*, referring to a coming time of spiritual awakening and planetary transition. Since the book was released in February of 1981, that affirmation has been echoed by thousands of activated Star People. We have been, quite literally, deluged by the mail response.

Star People research evolved from a rudimentary question-naire and an extensive series of personal interviews early in 1968. When Francie and I came together in 1975, she contributed several items of her own research, including the concept of the "Star Helpers," and our refined and blended investigation began in earnest early in 1976.

By the time *The Star People* was released, we knew with

utter certainty that "they" were out there. We were, though, unprepared for such an overwhelming response. Over a year since the book's publication, we are still averaging twenty letters a day from activated Star People—and some weeks we have received over seventy letters a day. Each trip to the mailbox has been like being bathed in love. We have often prompted unchecked tears as we read certain of the letters aloud to one another.

There are a number of basic themes that we have read over and over again:

"Thank God, you spoke up. I thought I was all alone down here!"

"Thank you for helping me to understand my true mission on Earth."

"Reading the book was like reading the story of my life."

"I am so happy that we are coming together as a Family."

"This book is an alarm clock for our species. I, too, know that 'Now is the Time.'"

Jennifer of Minneapolis wrote that, for her, reading *The Star People* was "sort of like reading a medical textbook, trying to self-diagnose what you have always thought was a horrible disease that you have and that you will surely die of one day—then finding out that your symptoms [referring to the Star People pattern profile] indicate that you are healthier and saner than you thought!"

For thousands of men and women, such as Pat, a writer from Los Angeles, the book provided memories that had long lain dormant in their psyches:

One summer night I woke up without reason to see a shining, silver humanoid being standing at the foot of my bed. I remember the sensation of undistilled terror. But the feeling changed into awe and wonder as I watched the being fade away.

The second event that I thought I had forgotten happened on Thanksgiving Day when I was either eleven or twelve. My father and I were driving home in the sleet after taking my [grandmother] home from her visit with us...We wound up on a lonely, dark, winding road, backward, because of the slick road surface.

Up to that point, my daddy and mother had taken care

of me . . . but that night, my father must have sensed he needed help, because he asked me to roll down my window and watch to make sure we didn't back off the edge. It was cold, and my face was numb and stinging, but I was exhilarated because I was needed . . .

Suddenly I saw directly behind us and just above us a brilliant white light with a bluish center. I did not hear a voice, but I was unmistakably getting a message from the light or from something. I knew somehow that [the message] was from myself—or from something connected with myself—in the future or in the past . . . I came away from that backward and downhill ride knowing with a deep certainty that "I am."

It was only years later that I found out what the "I am" phrase means in theology, in regard to Moses' experience with the burning bush. It's hard to put into words, but from that time on, I knew that "I was," that is, that I exist, that I will do so for all time, and that there has never been a time that I have not existed.

If even the archest of skeptics would read the mail from well-adjusted, well-educated, highly contributive men and women who freely claim such transcendental experiences, he would have to concede that "something is going on," that the individual mystical experience is far more widely spread than certain materialistic pundits would have us believe.

Integral to the Starseed is an activating visionary experience which occurs at about the age of five, introducing the child to an intelligence who thereby becomes a guiding entity and who maintains at least a sporadic contact with the Star Person throughout his or her life.

Art, a printer from Phoenix, was three years and nine months of age when he encountered his "Lady" on the beach one afternoon in June.

"Much has been lost and forgotten due to adults talking down my stories and giving me excuses for what I 'thought I saw,' " he told us. "The only thing I remember vividly was the loving feeling and the thought: 'You have so much to learn and so little time.' She repeated that statement over and over again—never actually speaking, but, rather, transmitting the thought while smiling."

Art's parents couldn't keep him in the house after that encounter with the Lady. He would crawl out of his window and lie on the porch roof most of the night. When they moved to a farm near Barstow, Illinois, he would sleep in the trees so that he might be nearer the stars.

Then, one night when he was eleven (another crucial age for Starseed), he and a friend were standing on a small bridge when a very bright object swooped down from the east and hovered over their heads.

"I tried to get my friend to look at it," Art remembers, "but he seemed in trance, so he did not see it."

Art began a quest on that evening that has taken him to nearly every part of the United States in search of more meaningful answers to life.

After his wife died in 1974, they continued an "exchange of wisdom" until his "Lady" arrived and took her to a "place of learning."

The Lady's last appearance to Art took place on April 17, 1979. Since then his teachings, warnings, and guidance have come from a male entity.

Art, just as so many Starseed, receives his transmissions "preceded by a pulsating buzz, a bright flash of light, then it's down to business—brief and to the point."

Art's son was born two and a half months premature, just as he himself had been. The boy walked and talked intelligently at the age of nine months. Then, when he was about four years old, he received nightly visits from the "Lady" for three weeks in June.

Because Art was receptive to his son's discussions of the visitations and because he encouraged the recitation of the transmissions, the child told him that the Lady had said that he "had much to learn in so little time." Supported by Art's interest, the child went on to relay the entity's teachings about death, the life beyond, and spiritual protection.

Christa had her life saved two times by three entities who guided her to safety as a child struggling for survival in Germany during World War II.

Once she was trapped in the cellar of her uncle's home, the survivor of a direct bomb hit. The entities, who at that time appeared as three bright lights, contacted Christa's grandparents in a mutual dream and caused them to insist that digging be resumed.

Later, the entities manifested in human form and motioned her off a bridge just before Allied bombs obliterated it.

Christa saw her first UFO when she was thirteen and living in Great Falls, Montana. The experience began her longing for the stars.

"I knew as I saw this UFO that I did not belong here on Terra [Earth]," she wrote. "Longingly, I wanted to go to my true home beyond our solar system. That night I was told in my dream that the time was not yet, and that I must grow and have patience."

In February of 1961, Christa "lost" five days of her life: "I remember a bright light, a control console and revolving crystals ... I had knowledge of a planet that was my true ancestral home."

She awakened fifteen miles from Great Falls. Five days had passed—although it seemed as if only five minutes had elapsed.

Christa soon discovered, however, that not only had she lost five days, she had also lost her job. And running through her thoughts was this bit of poetry:

> Lo and behold I enter your mind,
> and into your hands I deliver to you
> the body of a child!
> Born I know not where
> Conceived among the stars up there.
> Delivered to be raised by Terrans
> And to learn their ways
> Before returning back home
> To my ancestral race.

When he was four and a half, Boyd, presently personnel administrator for a Naval Reserve Center in Louisiana, was approached by a man in a robe and told that he would begin to learn how to teach on his fifth birthday. He was astonished when he read so many of the instructions that he had received from the entity to be also contained in *The Star People*.

As we reported in the earlier volume, 77 percent of the Starseeds claim to hear a whine, a click, or a buzzing sound preceding or during psychic events, warnings, messages, and so forth.

Amazingly, Francie and I read in letter after letter how this phenomenon actually drew the Starseed to find the books in stores and newsstands across the Americas and overseas. Here is a typical recounting of this mechanism at work:

> At the supermarket checkout they always have those romance novels and books which don't interest me in the least. But then I heard that sonic, mechanical whine that I often get in the back of my head. At that moment, I felt my body literally being taken over by force. Instinctively, my hand reached to a section of books and stretched in the back where I couldn't see. That's when I pulled out *The Star People*.

From February until nearly July of 1981, Francie and I attempted to answer each letter from the Star People personally—or to personalize with a brief note the eventual form letter that we were forced to devise. Many nights we would work until dawn, each of us answering a quota of seventy to eighty letters. We filed thousands of questionnaires and hundreds of exciting, inspiring, remarkably personal stories; and we tried our best to keep somehow abreast of the requests for additional information about the Star People.

In August of 1981, we were temporarily forced to cease the distribution of our Star People Questionnaire. We had no choice at that time other than to reply to queries with a form letter, stating frankly that we had exhausted the funds which we had set aside for research.

We have now resumed the distribution of the questionnaires, and we also wish to analyze more completely the new data which we have received from readers of the Star People series. We also would very much like to provide the services which the Star People have requested of us: a newsletter, development circles, study groups, and a national Star People center.

All these projects will have to wait, however, until such time as we receive adequate funding through royalties, endowments, donations, or whatever resources the Creative Energy will direct to us. Until we can afford to support such activities, we have decided that we must continue our mission of elevating awareness through our books, our tape cassettes, our instructional courses, and our seminars.

There is no question in our minds that the implications of the Star People research are staggering to conventional and orthodox thinkers. If a certain elasticity may be granted, we can state that an informal evaluation of the questionnaires and personal accounts received since publication of the book shows a fascinating substantiation of our earlier analyses of the Star People.

Certainly, the greater number of Star People continue to fit into the category of the "helpers" in our society. Perhaps the largest single category would be comprised of registered nurses, with psychologists, teachers, social workers, and psychic counselors not far behind. The number of chemists, physicists, and college professors identifying with the Star People pattern profile has been moving up in very rapid and impressive ways. And then there are housewives, farmers, truck drivers, and men and women from virtually every aspect of human endeavor. Whatever their line of work, the Star People are concerned with aiding and counseling their brothers and sisters as best they can.

A very important point to bring out is that both the Starseeds and the Star Helpers are independent thinkers, oriented toward individualized forms of spiritual expression. As a whole, the Star People are not joiners, belongers, or potential members of a cult. They appear to believe firmly in each person achieving his or her own path to the Source.

Our analyses before the publication of the book were based on about 35 percent men, 65 percent women. Interestingly, the immediate response to *The Star People* was heavily male. The flow balanced back to the female again, however, and we now have about 60 percent women and 40 percent men in our sampling of the Star People population.

The seeds responded in somewhat larger numbers, quite likely because they would experience the greater shock of recognition as they identified themselves in the book's listing of physical "symptoms." There is no way that we can state dogmatically what such things as extra vertebrae, unusual blood type, lower-than-normal body temperature actually mean; but once again, informally, we can now say that about 30 percent of those surveyed have extra or transitional vertebrae; 28 percent have unusual blood types; 19 percent have extra or transitional vertebrae *and* unusual blood types. Probably 95 percent have some kind of anomalous physical condition.

Chronic sinusitis seems more than ever to be one of the principal physical identifying factors of the seed—regardless of however bizarre that may seem. About 83 percent of the

Starseed suffer steadily from sinus trouble, while 87 percent
suffer from swollen or painful joints; 93 percent endure pain
in the back of the neck; and 84 percent are adversely affected
by high humidity.

At least 92 percent of the seed have lower-than-normal body
temperatures, and we now move up to about 75 percent of the
Starseed with low blood pressure. Well over 87 percent complain of hypersensitivity to sound, light, touch, colors, and
emotions.

Luana of Las Vegas writes that all of her senses are extended. In 1946–1947, a professor at the University of California in Los Angeles put her through a series of tests, utilizing
the facilities at UCLA. According to these reports:

> In the area of sight, my color perception extends in both
> directions, principally on the blue end.
>
> In hearing, the extension is such that any loud noise
> of prolonged duration—over thirty seconds—sets up a
> vibration which first causes pain in the mastoid area,
> then causes uncontrolled shaking which lasts for several
> minutes. The nerves of my entire body "jangle" and only
> subside when the noise ceases. It takes a good hour to
> return to normal, and I am wrung out. Sirens are a con-
> stant menace. Thank goodness they do not last for very
> long at a time.

A retired schoolteacher, Luana recalled that one of her worst
experiences with noise occurred in the school parking lot when
all the drivers began honking their car horns to celebrate a
sports victory.

> It took fifteen minutes to get away from the noise, and
> a half an hour before I could get control and get out of
> the car. It took a stiff drink to dull my nerves to a
> semblance of normality.

Luana's taste tests demonstrated her ability to detect minute
quantities of sweet or sour. And as are so many Star People,
she is hypersensitive to alcohol, several types of medication,
and most drugs.

Bright light is a hazard. In 1962, standing in the sun, perceiving flashes off band instruments, caused a temporary blindness. My students led me back to class. It took about half an hour for sight to return. . . .

Emotions create problems for Star People because they are so empathic. In order to function effectively as counselors, they must learn to create shells around themselves. As Luana remembered it:

At one time in my mid-twenties, it was necessary for me to escape from my friends whose problems and joys I absorbed to such an extent that I was physically drained . . . It was also at that time that I learned to seal my emotions off and no longer absorb so much. There have still been recent times when I have been physically drained by the problems or excitement of others, but the renewal is rapid.

Cliff of Gainesville, Florida, expresses the hypersensitivity to light, touch, emotion, and hearing, but he has found some compensation in a response that other Star People have also noted: "When I kiss or make love, I hear music coming from the other person and/or myself."

Sensitivity to vibrations considered "musical" by those in the physical plane is also a common factor in the Star People pattern profile, especially for those, like Cliff, who are visited by such entities as a "music-voiced girl-woman who radiates shining white light."

Consistent with our earlier figures, the Starseed are at least 87 percent "night people," who prefer to do their most important mental or creative work after sundown.

In our broader sampling of Starseeds, we find that about 94 percent of them vividly recall their activating experience with an entity or light manifestation at about the age of five, while the other six percent are consciously aware that "something important" happened to them at that time.

Nearly all the seeds remember always yearning for a place that they consider their "true home," somewhere not on Earth. A good many of the Star Helpers, while not evidencing the physical characteristics of the Starseed, also expressed a similar yearning.

One of the seeds said that he had spent so much time looking for the "picture in my mind" that he had earned the nickname of "Tumbleweed." His quest has led him to travel "forty-nine states and Canada."

But, he continued, "Ever since 1971, something has been drawing me toward the eastern midsection of Arizona. I know it's very close now."

As previously suggested, about 88 percent of the Starseeds are empaths, and we have now learned that so are about 72 percent of the Star Helpers.

Nearly 100 percent of the Starseeds experience a feeling of great urgency to accomplish important goals, and about 93 percent of the Star Helpers share that inner prompting. Approximately 85 percent of the Starseeds have been altered by their guidance that "Now is the Time" to begin working against a cosmic timetable, and about 74 percent of the Star Helpers have received the same alert.

It must be continually emphasized that in our discussion of "seeds" and "helpers" that we are by no means speaking of some exclusive clubs of "chosen people." If anything, we are observing the formulation of a worldwide service organization, dedicated to lighting candles rather than cursing the darkness.

Although one cannot grow an extra vertebrae or any of the other anomalous physical expressions of the Starseed, one can certainly work toward developing the Star Consciousness which both the seeds and the helpers manifest in their personal lives. An extra rib, an unusual blood type, is but an enigma, with no understandable purpose of this moment in time and space. But Star Consciousness—call it cosmic consciousness, Christ consciousness, if you will—is of inestimable value to all of humankind.

Any sincere person may become a Star Person by undertaking a program of study, self-discipline, balance, meditation, and awareness techniques. A dedicated regimen of going within to link up with the Greater Reality may spark Star Consciousness and a sense of responsibility toward one's fellow humans and to all other life forms on the planet. It is such an inner prompting that provokes Star People on their mission to be light bearers and to shine their spiritual lights so that all may see their individual paths to the Source more clearly.

Neither are we insistent on the term "Star People" to designate the seeds of the New Humanity which are blossoming forth all over the world. Star People is a designation that is comfortable and symbolic for us.

In the November 1980 issue of *Mystical World*, S.A. Ryan used the term "Catalyst Soul" before she knew *The Star People* was "in the works." According to Ms. Ryan's concepts:

The world needs Catalysts [an element that can cause change], now more than ever before. The Catalyst Soul is used by God to spur others on toward their fullest potential, and at times, to nudge people into fulfilling their karma.

The Catalyst is never bored . . . In times of quiet, the entity is possessed of an inner strength that lies beneath the surface. There are also periods of what seem to be "hyperactivity." Like a battery, the Catalyst has a positive and a negative pole. The energy within can only be loosed when proper contact is made with the needful recipient.

. . . Needy people gravitate toward these individuals to seek out counsel and to unload cares and troubles. [The Catalysts] are "God's listeners" . . . and the confused or weakened souls are attracted, like bees to pollen, to gather strength and insight. . . .

Catalysts rarely mince words, for they don't waste time worrying about keeping large armies of casual friends; in fact, usually the entity can count his or her true friends on one hand. Personal loneliness is likely to be the lot of this helper soul. The people who take or receive guidance from the Catalyst seldom give thought to just how desperate they were before they drew energy from their helper. They seldom remember to . . . give thanks. . . . It is assumed that the Catalyst has no "need." After all, *he* has it all together, or *she* is so fortunate!

. . . There is no age group or profession particularly accented; in fact, I have often seen in the [astrological] charts of the newborn that a "little Catalyst" has come into the lives of the family. . . . I have found that Catalysts are aggressive and action-oriented.

Many so-called "hyper" individuals are not nervous

at all! They are simply on a different wave length. They
accomplish a great deal for their minds are operating in
a multilevel manner. Instead of *despairing* of that young-
ster, *understand* the child! Share the interests and provide
the tools for growth. Too many of our talented youngsters
are forced into roles of normalcy when they could be
soaring to wondrous heights. . . .

. . . Many Catalyst individuals, after searching their
memories, attest to an accident that resulted in uncon-
sciousness, a blow to the head, or an illness that caused
an extremely high temperature. The general timing of
these traumas most often coincide with years one, seven,
fourteen to fifteen, and twenty to twenty-one.

It is my feeling that changes, triggered at these times,
open the consciousness to objectivity. This, in turn, al-
lows the individual to rise above making purely emotional judgments when confronted with a dilemma.
Traumas can occur at any time in life with these same
results, but it is apparent that the rough increments of
seven years are the ones most mentioned. Often, "out-
of-body" experiences are described in connection with
the trauma.

Is it reasonable to take seriously the [Catalysts'] repeated descriptions of a "being of light" explaining that
"There is still work to be done on Earth"? I believe it
is! I have heard too many of these accounts, with minor
variations, to discard the information as mere dream experience.

Ms. Ryan's research is but one of dozens which were sent
to us by Star People who had begun to receive their own visions,
inspirations, and investigations of the global phenomenon before they read our book.

In 1976, long before she had knowledge of our Star People
premise, Laurie was corresponding with a friend on "being
different." She decided, in the expression of a poem, that they
were "Star People":

There are those whom others say
Live in a world of their own,
Whose eyes do not always see what is before them,
But something invisible, beyond.

They are the ones who dare nurture dreams—
Fragile crystals displayed
For the scrutiny of a scornful world. . . .


. . . On clear nights you may glimpse them,
Upturned faces bathed in pale starlight,
Gazing as if their very souls
Were mirrored in those tiny, shimmering jewels—
As, indeed, they are.

These are the new generations,
Whose lives are compelled toward goals even they
    would not believe.
Envy them not, for their days are filled with pain and
    frustration;
but neither mock them, for their visions are the seeds
    of humankind's future.

Stephanie of Youngstown, Ohio, wrote down her concept
of "Cosmic People" in 1980 when, according to her letter, she
was "one full year away from reading your enlightening and
stunning book."

Stephanie commented to us that "as with probably everyone
else that you have heard from, I, too, was shocked to discover
that thousands of people have been contacted by Light Beings;
I was also completely amazed that so many people have been
given the same types of ideas and messages from their sky
families. It truly is wonderful and wondrous!"

Stephanie told us of her encounter with two Sky Beings at
age five which altered her life from that moment onward. As
her quest continued, she, too, had become interested in doc-
umenting the awakening of the "Cosmic People."

As in the case of our own research, Stephanie commented:
"They do not originate in any one group of human beings; they
seem to come from every race, color, creed, nationality, philosophy, psychology, and political belief on the face of the
Earth. However, they hold certain ideas and ideals in common
within their hearts. . . ."

Here, considerably abbreviated, are Stephanie's guidelines
for identifying the "Cosmic People":

(1) Cosmic People have a definite sense of mission in
this world . . . They go through life with the intention of

making it better for everyone . . . They build up, rather than tear down, create rather than destroy, help rather than hinder, and give rather than receive.

(2) . . . They are interested, involved people who are fascinating as well as fascinated. They take part in this world . . . They are busy trying to make a difference.

(3) Cosmic People look to the heavens for their "raison d'être." They somehow know in their hearts that they originate there, they belong there, and most importantly, someday they will be there again . . . This knowledge gives their whole lives meaning, direction, force, power. They know intuitively where they're going from where they've been.

(4) Cosmic People know that racial, religious, or political prejudice can claim no part of their attention or interest . . . No cause is holy enough to justify holocaust and annihilation. . . .

(5) Cosmic People allow their psychic natures to grow and develop . . . They know that these [abilities] are normal and natural in the scheme of things, and they keep them in balance and utilize them in moderation. . . .

(6) Cosmic People usually feel as if they've had a number of past lives, and they therefore generally believe in some form of reincarnation. . . .

(7) Cosmic People [emanate] an aura of kindness, gentleness, goodness . . . However, they don't feel driven to proselytize for what they believe in, knowing that those who will eventually feel the same as they will come to do so on their own. . . .

(8) The Cosmic People accept in-dream visitations, reports and sightings of UFOs, and actual close encounters as real, natural, and normal . . . They feel fortunate to have had these experiences happen to them, and they look forward to possible future visitations; but they do not ruin their entire present lives by waiting for such experiences and doing little else besides.

(9) The Cosmic People respect present-day science and industry and don't feel unduly frustrated when these entities are "slow" to progress. . . .

(10) The Cosmic People read, write, see, talk about, promote, and love excellent pieces of science, fantasy, and science fiction entertainment and information. . . .

Betty of Tucson, Arizona, told us that she was a sixty-five-year-old mother who had given birth to a nest of six *seed*lings and *star*lings. Proudly, she delineated the four who had full awareness of who they were and why they were here: Number One, a forty-five-year-old male, a nuclear physicist; Number Two, a forty-three-year-old male, a Commander in the United States Navy; Number Three, a female, thirty-two, who was an opthalmic technician; and Number Six, a twenty-six-year-old housewife and mother.

Betty was far from discouraged about her other two. Number Four, she told us, was a thirty-one-year-old female, an artist, who had just had her first UFO sighting. And, she mused, Number Five, a twenty-nine-year-old male technologist, just hadn't been able yet to define his destiny.

The Starseed are not without their frustrations in dealing with this Earth, as Frederike of Pasadena, California, confessed to us:

> Let me say that your books, meditations, and so forth, are helping me to rid myself of much anger at the people who are messing about with the Earth . . . Sometimes, much to my shame (I don't like admitting this to you!) I think, "Why should we help these idiots? These people who kill and tear and hurt things without so much as a thought of regret are barely out of the mud. Just let them go!"
>
> This is not a very enlightened thought on my part, is it? I know, and deeply, too, that we have an obligation to help everyone—and most especially those people who are living in the dark and who are ignorant when they destroy Earth's gifts and resources and all the other things they mess up . . .

Jack, a U.S. Coast Guard electronics technician, from Morro Bay, California, has experienced "visions of an infinitely expanding universe" since his early childhood. He also expressed to us his occasional feelings of sadness in living among largely insensitive men and women who express too much of the Earth, and too little of the stars:

> It is difficult for me to find people who are willing to drop their daily schedules and thoughts and work and

social conglomerations to just experience the magic of life and spirit with a fellow human. Alas, this tends to dampen my enthusiasm at times, and I pick up too much of the oppression which surrounds me.

Occasionally, though, there is the fresh breeze of the exceptional individual who blows in from the depths of humanity. At those times I rejoice.

Somehow, it seems, the Star People always manage to keep their optimism about the missions that have been Soul-chosen for them.

Virginia is currently a technician with the Air Force, but she remembers that her activating experience occurred on a Christmas Eve when she was about four. The incident was highlighted by an out-of-body experience when Virginia got up and "walked" to see the Christmas tree lights, then saw her still-sleeping body lying in bed.

I knew that if I woke up then, it would still be Christmas Eve and I would still be four years old. Then I knew, somehow, that even if I didn't wake up until years later, like Sleeping Beauty, nothing would change. It's really funny, but that incident formed my entire approach and attitude toward life. I know that, somewhere, I'm still four years old, and it will always be Christmas Eve.

Regardless of whether or not they might be blessed with such an insightful and restorative personal vision, the Star People know that they can always rejuvenate their energies through meditation. Dale of Waltham, Massachusetts, uses a crystal to go deep within her psyche and to return with such expressions of the experience as the following:

Seas of brilliant colors, flowing and swelling, moving like graceful wings.
Energy surrounds my whole being.
My mind grows even stronger, and I am filled with the light of a thousand suns.
I feel totally alive, rejuvenated, and renewed.
Purples burst from my eyes; blues and golds swirl from my hands.
I live.

I am the Light, eternally guiding others to my father,
Growing brighter and brighter,
bursting and rising into the far reaches of the
Universe.
To the place of beginnings . . .
Home!

# Chapter Eight

## THE X-FORCE: A TRANS-FORMATIVE ENERGY

> Real then to the man who has had contact with it or lives in it, is the cosmic consciousness, with a greater than physical reality; real in itself, real in its effects and works.
> *Sri Aurobindo*

The Hindus call it *prana*. The Chinese name it *chi*. The Japanese identify it as *ki*. The Hawaiian Huna priests recognize it as *mana*. The Norse blend with it as *wodan*. The Plains Indians chant its name as *wakan*. The Hebrew tradition knows it as *Ruah*. The Christians welcome it as the *Holy Spirit*.

All cultures at one time or another have sensed an unknown energy which underlies all paranormal phenomena and which is an essential part of all life on this planet. Throughout history, thousands upon thousands of Starseed have understood that the ability to control this energy lies dormant within their psyches. Unselfishly, they have tried to make all evolved and sensitive men and women understand that the X-Force is also accessible to them.

Our friend Komar (Vernon Craig) was activated through dream-teachings as a child and has experienced contact with multidimensional beings as an adult. Komar channels the energy of his cosmic heritage by controlling pain through altered states of consciousness, then he strives to teach others how to accomplish these mind-over-matter abilities.

Komar has been listed as a master of physical feats in the *Guinness Book of Records*, and he is holder of several world records in endurance and pain control. In addition to lying on beds of nails, surviving the press of great weights, and bending steel bars with his bare hands, Komar can demonstrate his Starseeded potential to the extent of walking on beds of red coals at temperatures as high as 1500 degrees F. to the satisfaction of committees of medical doctors and scientists.

Some years ago, we asked Dr. Norman Shealy of the Pain Rehabilitation Center, St. Francis Hospital, La Crosse, Wisconsin, to examine Komar thoroughly. Contained within Dr. Shealy's extensive report was the following analysis: "It is obvious that Komar has the ability to distract his mind by going into at least an alpha state of consciousness—and in it to have control over his autonomic nervous system. Komar uses this state of mind to prevent pain and body damage."

What Komar really seeks to accomplish in his public demonstrations is to provide a shock effect that will excite people into realizing that they live their entire existences without using more than ten-to-twenty percent of their full mental capacities. Komar is challenging everyone that if he can utilize a portion of that dormant eighty percent of brainpower, so can we!

Komar, and many other Star People of great physical abilities, are demonstrating that the conduit for the X-Force—the *mana*, the *prana*, the *chi*—is the human psyche.

We are in contact with several Starseed and Star Helpers who have genuine abilities to bend metal, move thimbles across glass plates, and even to materialize and dematerialize objects—all by utilizing the X-Force, not tricks and gimmicks. From time to time, they are confronted by publicity-hungry professional magicians who announce that they can replicate anything that the true psychic sensitives can accomplish.

Once when a magician claimed that he could duplicate Komar's firewalking prowess, my friend told me, "I would love to see him follow me across a bed of coals stoked up to 1500 degrees. His feet wouldn't look like a baby's bottom when he got through the way mine do. He'd have nothing left but charred stumps! His phoney magic wouldn't stand up to my real magic on a bed of coals."

No contest between Real Magician and professional trickster ever materialized. Instead, the challenger gave a demonstration of skillful footwork on boards placed among smoldering lumber and explained away Komar's abilities as being but an exhibition of similar trickery. It must always be remembered that, by the very nature of their trade, magicians are professional liars.

Unfortunately, the average man and woman does have a great deal of difficulty in deciding what is real or unreal among the claims of genuine and alleged psychic sensitives and the accusations of professional magicians. In our day of scientific wonders, there exist few things that cannot be replicated—or appear to be replicated.

Generations of men and women have become conditioned to seeing ghosts, monsters, and spaceships in the movie theaters and on their television sets. Attractive witches wiggle their cute noses and objects fly across the room. Captain Kirk gives the command to be beamed aboard the *Enterprise*, and he, Spock, and Dr. McCoy dematerialize and rematerialize before our eyes.

But just as the most beautifully wrought artificial rose does not negate the reality of a real rose, neither does the artificially wrought presentation of psychic phenomena negate the reality of real psychic manifestations. There truly are real roses amidst all the artificial ones.

Whether spontaneously or through disciplined training, psychic sensitives have learned to control the same Unknown Energy of which certain adepts were aware thousands of years ago. The Algonquin's *Manitou*, the Sufis' *Baraka*, Plato's *Nous*, Aristotle's Formative Cause are all names, terms, and concepts which epitomize humankind's persistent attempts to identify and to define the energy that the more sensitive of the species have always known existed around them.

In some way, the human psyche serves as a conduit for this energy that, in turn, enables telepathy, psychokinesis, prophesy, clairvoyance, levitation, and so forth, to be manifested.

Those bold-thinking scientists who have begun attempts to isolate the X-Force had first to begin to apprehend consciousness as a nonphysical, but very real, quality. And they had to understand that physical reality is connected to consciousness by means of a single physically fundamental element—the Unknown Energy.

Science long ago discovered that everything is vibration. Everything, no matter how solid it may appear to humankind's physical senses, is vibrating at its own particular frequency. Every human being, every animal, every band of metal sends out short waves of different lengths. What is more, these personal wave lengths are as individual as fingerprints.

It has been discovered that within every living organism there exists an energy, which, however weak, however unpredictable, can be refracted, polarized, focused, and combined with other energies. Sometimes it seems as though this energy has effects similar to those of magnetism, electricity, heat, and luminous radiation—yet it truly appears to be none of these things.

Perhaps the Unknown Energy is that agent of which the great French Magus Eliphas Levi referred when he wrote:

> There exists an agent which is natural and divine, material and spiritual, a universal plastic mediator, a common receptacle of the vibrations of motions and the images of form, a fluid and a force, which may be called in some way the Imagination of Nature. The existence of this force is the *Great Arcanum* of practical Magick.

As an intriguing paradox to the current analyses of science it may be said that while the Unknown Energy is often observed in the operation of heat, light, electricity, magnetism, and chemical reactions, it is somehow different from all of those known forces and energies. It appears to fill all of space, penetrating and permeating everything. Interestingly, denser materials seem to conduct it better and faster. Metal refracts it. Organic material absorbs it.

The X-Force is basically synergetic, which, simply stated, means that it has a very cooperative energy—one that blends well with other energies. It is so cooperative that things with which it might come into contact do not disintegrate or disorganize the way they normally would.

Therefore, it might be said that the X-Force has a basic negentropic effect, which makes it the opposite of entropy, the expected disintegration and disorganization of matter. Somehow, the X-Force manages to violate the Second Law of Thermodynamics. It has a formative and an organizing effect. Just as heat increases, so does the effect of the X-Force.

Such a phenomenon has often been observed when a psychic

sensitive bends a fork, a spoon, or a band of metal by psychokinesis, mind over matter. The metals continue to bend
long after the sensitive has touched them.

In certain experiments seeking to photograph the X-Force
around psychic men and women with highly sensitized film,
it was found that the life-giving, synergistic energy is blue in
color. The entropic, disintegrative energy, on the other hand,
has been photographed as yellowred. It has also been discovered that the synergistic energy projects a cool, pleasant feeling,
while the entropic energy projects a feeling of heat and un-
pleasantness.

It would also appear that plants, animals, humans, and crystals contain within themselves a series of geometrical points in
which the energy of the X-Force can become highly concentrated. Such points seem to respond to the chakras, of which
the Yogis spoke; for, in humans, they are located at the top of
the head, between the eyebrows, the throat, the heart, the
spleen, the solar plexus, the base of the spine, and the genitals.

It seems to be just as the ancient mystery schools and the
psychic sensitives have always told us, albeit in slightly different words: The energies somehow flow from one object to
another.

The Polynesian Kahunas tell us that the X-Force is sticky,
thereby enabling an *aka* cord, or an invisible stream of energy,
to connect any two objects that have in any way been connected
in the past.

Such a belief has, of course, been the very essence of sympathetic magic—that one can establish communication with,
or gain information about, or do harm or healing, to someone
by contact with an object previously associated with him.

Psychic sensitives have claimed to be able to see the X-
Force as isolated, pulsating points of light; as spirals; or as
clouds or auras surrounding the human body or an object with
which a living thing has come into direct contact. When a
psychic sensitive projects the X-Force outward, toward others,
it can be used for healing.

And what of those practitioners of darker Magic, those ma-
nipulators of unseen forces?

Might they project the X-Force for negative purposes, to
hurt people?

Might they practice Voodoo, hexes, Black Magic?

Proper application of the X-Force depends upon the spiritual status and the intention of the practitioner. That is why I believe that an emphasis must always be placed upon the God-link, so that the Unknown Energy is used only for good.

But as long as we are on the Earth Plane in a three-dimensional world, we must recognize the fact that, like electricity, the X-Force may be used for both positive or negative accomplishments.

The X-Force, of itself, is neither good nor evil. Electricity is neither good nor evil of itself. We all know, however, that electricity can be used to warm our breakfast toast, heat our homes, and light up our cities. It can also be used to project violent and pornographic films, broadcast the propaganda of prejudice, and electrocute someone.

At some level of the universe, the X-Force blends and interconnects each of us to the other—and to all living things on the planet. On some level of consciousness, every living cell is in communication with every other living cell.

Currently, many scientists of consciousness are finding the hologram to be a workable analogy to illustrate such a concept of the Oneness of things.

What is most truly remarkable about a hologram is that every single part of it contains all the information about the whole, just as the DNA in each cell of the body contains the blueprint for the entire physical structure. Split a hologram in half, shine a laser through it, and the whole object is reconstituted in three dimensions.

The human brain seems to be holographic in the manner in which it stores memory. Destroy one part of the brain, and the memory survives in others.

It has been postulated that the entire universe may be a single hologram. It may well be that information about all of it is encapsulated in each part of it.

And that includes each of us human beings. We may all be unfolded images of aspects which exist in a higher reality.

Physicist David Bohm of the University of London deals with the matter in his book, *Wholeness and the Implicate Order*, in which he urges each of us to become aware that the modern view of the world has become fragmented, especially in the sciences, but also in the execution of our daily lives. In science's desire to divide our universe into stars and atoms, it separated us from nature. In humankind's prejudice of dividing itself into races, nations, political parties, and economic classes, it fragmented us from any underlying wholeness with each other.

"It is not an accident," Dr. Bohm observes, "that our fragmentary form of thought is leading to such a widespread range of crises, social, political, economic, ecological, psychological, etc., in the individual and in society as a whole. Such a mode of thought implies unending development of chaotic and meaningless conflict, in which the energies of all tend to be lost by movements that are antagonistic or else at cross-purposes."

The visions and inner-teachings of the Starseed have convinced them that there is a remarkable biological transformation that is taking place now in all of humankind. Some turn of the great Wheel of Destiny, some advent of a New Age on the great Cosmic Calendar, has caused the X-Force to circulate in certain members of humankind.

Some are awakening to the impulses of the cosmic seed within them. Some are suffering from internal tensions and subliminal fears beyond their understanding, as the entire species moves toward a time of transition. What the Star People wish to manifest most of all are ways in which they might better teach balance and harmony to all of humankind.

The controlled manipulation of the X-Force may become more valuable to humankind than the discovery of fire, electricity, and nuclear energy. It may enable humankind to control virtually any and all environmental requirements, thereby elevating men and women above physical considerations and catapulting them into more spiritual dimensions.

I must refer now to my friends and associates who are working in the new-old science of psychotronics or radionics and who are utilizing incredible devices such as the Hieronymous Machine. It is they who are currently doing the most productive work in harnessing the X-Force.

T. Galen Hieronymous was a pioneer radio operator and electrical engineer, who participated in the first radio broadcast in 1913 when he was with station KDKA in Pittsburgh. Hieronymous patented his strange, little "black box" in 1948, primarily as an instrument for detecting new and unknown emanations from inert matter.

It was George De La Warr, who, in about 1955, made the

incredible discovery that the emulsion on a photographic plate could be somehow linked to someone who has had his picture taken.

Or, it must be added, linked to places and things that have had their pictures taken.

By using the Hieronymous Machine and a psychic sensitive at its dials, for example, infested crops thousands of miles distant have been rid of yield-robbing insects. Fruit trees have been divested of parasitic infection while the black box and the manipulator sat nearly half a continent away from them.

As it was explained to me by a psychotronic enthusiast in Chicago: "All we need is a photograph, with the negative, of any infected grove of trees or field of crops. We insert the photograph in the well of the box and instruct the medium, the psychic sensitive, to turn the dial until it gets 'sticky.' That's when he or she has picked up the parasite's vibrations. Then that's it. The area is cleaned of the insect or the worm almost immediately, even if the field or grove is thousands of miles away from us."

Another radionics expert, a former diplomat from an Oriental nation, added the following startling information: "If we have a photograph and the negative of someone who needs healing, we insert the photograph in the well of the machine, and we ask the psychic to turn the dial until he or she feels the frequency of that person. As with the killing of insects, so it is with healing. Cures may be accomplished almost at once, even if the subject may be halfway around the world."

How can such a thing be possible from a photograph or a drop of blood?

Science has learned that each individual molecule of matter has within it an electrical charge that is specific for that particular molecule. That unique electrical charge may be compared to a miniscule radio station that is capable of sending and receiving its own particular signals. When these countless numbers of charged molecules are transmitting, they are in the process of building up a generic pattern which is the procedure that enables a shape to appear in the material dimension.

For instance, the separate "broadcasts" of the billions of charged molecules in a tulip combine into one signal which is unique. And each of the other tulips in the flower bed is not quite the same as it is. Every one of them has its own unique broadcast of charged molecules, and each of those miniscule molecules is a receiver, as well as a transmitter.

When we take a picture of something, the psychotronic scientists theorize, the film emulsion manages to retain the generic pattern of the subject being photographed. If we place the photograph in such a device as a Hieronymous Machine and focus the X-Force upon it, the generic pattern that has been captured by the emulsion will transmit the exact pattern of radiation which will enable us to affect the tulip, the insect, or the person at a distance.

Is it really possible that every single molecule is like a tiny radio set that can both send and receive?

The radionics experts believe that to be the case. And they theorize that the molecule broadcasts ceaselessly and on many different wavelengths—but only on *one* frequency at a time.

There seems to be some way in which the Hieronymous Machine—and any other so-called "radionics machine"—utilizes the X-Force to stimulate the psyche of the operator to form a connection with the molecules of matter in the generic pattern of the subject.

James B. Beal is a former NASA engineer whose avocation of investigating unexplained phenomena in the realms of parapsychology and paraphysics has enabled him to become very knowledgeable about such matters as psychotronics.

"These devices [the Hieronymous Machine, De La Warr Radionic Diagnostic Instrument, the Pavlita Psychotronic Generators, etc.] perform no understood function by themselves, based on our present understanding of physics," Beal writes. "All of these devices seem to incorporate symbolic relationships of one sort or another. Patterns are present for concentration and/or touch and focus of some sort of complex mental biological energy. Relationships of texture, shape, arrangement, materials, and size seem important only in order to achieve some sort of optimum 'resonant' condition."

Beal observes that such devices also offer a placebo effect to the practitioner. In these days of science and gadget worship, it is easy to give credit for something not understood to a machine—"because such talents are 'impossible' for ordinary human beings due to their cultural conditioning."

People who have been operating psychotronic devices for several years begin to use them less and less, Beal notes.

"If the operation of these devices relates to the symbolic, then why shouldn't one set up a relationship pattern among the neurons of the brain that can do the job as well?"

Why not indeed? Such a relationship pattern among the neurons of the brain would constitute True Magick, just as the serious practitioner has been using it for centuries. This marvelous internal gift of healing and transformation may be one of the essential teachings which the Star Gods came to this planet to impart to humankind.

In his paper, "The Ethical Use of Psychic Energy," Duane Elgin of Stanford Research Institute writes that "consciousness can manifest as a form of energy, which in turn can manifest in or act upon matter."

In this view, consciousness is more than a biochemical phenomenon confined to our bodies. Consciousness is also a force or energy that partakes of a nonphysical realm unbounded by the constraints of linear time and three-dimensional space.

If the foregoing is true, the act of mobilizing our consciousness becomes an act of psychic functioning that may impinge directly upon the universe along the entire continuum of reality—from consciousness to energy to matter. Thus, anyone who is capable of directing his consciousness with intense focus and concentration should, hypothetically, be capable of significant psychic functioning.

At this point, the question might once again be raised whether the consciousness of one person, intensely focused and concentrated, could be used negatively upon another.

"Everyone hates to bring that subject up," one of the psychotronic experts admitted to me. "The answer is a qualitative, 'yes,' for we do not yet know to what extent a human can be affected negatively by the X-Force."

But what about the ridding of thousands of acres of farmland of insects and pests?

"The operator must be a moral person," he answered reflectively. "He or she must be one who continually strives for balance."

A psychic sensitive who had served as the operator in several psychotronic experiments told me that she always prayed for guidance before she began turning the dial on the Hieronymous Machine.

"We begin each session by visualizing a circle of white light around us," she continued. "The very act of visualizing such a shield encourages the energy to form a barrier between the operator and any external negativity."

The radionics researcher who employed the psychic sensitive spoke up: "The energy seems to be malleable in that way. It can be shaped and directed by the mind.

"I am convinced that the X-Force is not related to alpha or beta particles or to gamma rays. As far as I can ascertain at this point in my research, it does not seem to fit into any part of the electromagnetic spectrum. I think it operates in an entirely different, previously unknown medium."

In addition to visualizing circles of white light, I wanted to know if there were other methods by which we might protect ourselves from an unbalanced intelligence directing the X-Force in a purposefully negative way.

If a positive control of the Unknown Energy can be one of the most powerful and effective means of achieving both the elevation of awareness and the constructive manipulation of physical matter on this planet, then we must be mindful of the laws of polarity which also operate on Earth. After all, if the Star People are concentrating on doing good, might we not assume from the evidence contained in every daily newspaper and on every newsbroadcast that others are concentrating on doing evil?

I asked Francie to channel some answers for me regarding the proper utilization of the X-Force, and the most effective ways of protecting oneself from evil. Here are her responses to my questions:

Those things which we call "evil" are basically negative applications of the survival mechanisms of Animal Man. For instance, that which is now termed "lust" was once necessary to perpetuate the species. That which is now called "greed" often permitted individuals to survive under adverse conditions in the primitive state.

Those things which we call evil have no external origin. They come from within. They are the result of the friction between the Animal Self and the Spiritual Self within each member of humankind. Only those who harbor the seed of Christ consciousness are able to rise above this inevitable friction; and they become the greatest of our spiritual teachers, saints, and holy ones.

Awareness negates evil. Awareness means accepting responsibility for one's action. That which we call "sin" occurs when one shuns awareness in favor of Animal-Self expression.

To blame such actions upon an external devil is to avoid personal responsibility.

Evil is never stronger than good. Evil prevails on Earth because it is permitted to do so by humankind's general lack of awareness, for even those who strive for enlightenment often make choices which better serve the Animal Self.

It is true that the X-Force can be used on Earth for either good or evil. As one raises his awareness, it becomes less likely that the X-Force will be used negatively. It is impossible for the enlightened who receive from the higher planes of existence to use the energy for anything other than good.

Those who use the X-Force for personal gain and the exploitation of others cannot use it everlastingly to harm those who work for good. Evil works most effectively against those who do evil. The good, the innocent, are always capable of repelling negative applications of the X-Force.

Evil presently prevails on Earth, because it is linked. Evil is directed by the collective energy of the conscious preference of the great masses of people for the requirements of the Animal Self over those desires of the Spirit Self.

Good is ultimately superior, and even now that which we term Evil cannot of itself directly conquer Good. Evil can presently dominate Good only if the one yielding to Animal Self also yields to the physical expression of violence. It is only when Evil is coupled with physical violence that it can temporarily suppress Good. Those who do Evil, however, can prosper on only a short-term basis.

While it is true that those who have immersed themselves in negativity can, for a time, become the "Lords of the Earth," their kingdom is a very transient one, for it is material, rather than spiritual.

It is not true that it is only the wicked who prosper. Those who serve Good may utilize the X-Force and come to prosper in the here-and-now. They need not wait for their "treasures in Heaven," if they but balance their actions with love and continue to elevate themselves spiritually.

# Chapter Nine

## DARK SHADOWS IN THE MAGIC THEATER

We have found that where science has progressed the farthest, the mind has but regained from nature that which the mind put into nature. We have found a strange footprint on the shores of the unknown. We have devised profound theories, one after another, to account for its origin. At last we have succeeded in reconstructing the creature that made the footprint. And lo! It is our own.

*Sir Arthur Eddington*

Dr. Henry Lazarus'* involvement with the paranormal and his first discovery of the X-Force began when he became interested in UFOs.

Although he had pooh-poohed "flying saucers" in a kind of orthodox reflex action, he had occasion one weekend in October of 1971 to be staying at a hotel in Chicago where a UFO conference was being held. He had been amused by some of the conventioneers in the lobby—men with antennae fixed to their heads, spacey-eyed women dressed in flowing gowns—but then he chanced to glance at the program roster.

In addition to questionable presentations on visits to Venus and conversations with flying saucer pilots, he was surprised

*In this chapter I have changed names, altered places, and dramatized certain aspects of the cases for what will soon be revealed as obvious reasons.

to see the names of a number of rather prominent astronomers, physicists, psychiatrists, and authors who were scheduled to give lectures on what seemed to be *bona fide* subjects relative to speculations on extraterrestrial visitations to Earth.

He had a few hours to kill, so he decided to buy some tickets and listen to a couple of the more lucid sounding speeches. He could, after all, leave in three minutes if his scientific sensibilities should be offended.

Not only did he become intrigued, rather than insulted, he found that he had become hooked by the whole area of UFO research.

His credentials easily bought him access to an all-night bull session with those members of the scientific community who dared association with the lunatic fringe in order to pursue an area of inquiry which they were convinced was of paramount importance to the planet's continued existence. Lazarus found that he was totally enthralled by these men and women who had immersed themselves in a field of research that challenged the scientific paradigm of the twentieth century.

Henry Lazarus' next step had been to fly to Boston to proselytize UFOs to his old friend Benjamin Chiang, an esteemed university professor of physics. Chiang had always been one of the most open-minded individuals whom Lazarus had ever encountered, and his response to Lazarus' presentation of the subject had been customarily direct. Instead of relying upon secondary reports, why did they not travel to a scene of alleged UFO activity and collect their own primary data?

Lazarus was pleased with his friend's reasonable suggestion, and he was excited by the proximity of such an area of alleged phenomena. One of the researchers at the Chicago conference had told him of a small town not far from Springfield, Massachusetts, where it was claimed that UFO manifestations could be observed almost nightly. The town was situated on the Connecticut River in the Holyoke Mountain Ridge, and it was only a few hours' drive from Boston.

Chiang had only a morning class on Wednesday, the next day. Why procrastinate? They could be on the road before noon and arrive on the scene in plenty of time to witness whatever activity the UFOnauts had in store for them. Since his first class on Thursday was not until after lunch, they could afford the time to stay overnight if the phenomena put in a late appearance.

Chiang asked if Henry would mind if they asked a friend of his, a very skeptical, hard-nosed professor of biology, to accompany them if his schedule were compatible with such an expedition. In true scientific spirit, Lazarus welcomed a closed mind as a kind of control.

Two hours outside of Boston on the following day, Henry had begun to regret extending his permission to invite Dr. Philip Reisman along on the excursion. Reisman was more than a skeptic, he was a cynic. But it was fall, a beautiful October day, and the dazzling display of leaves in the brilliant autumn colors enabled Lazarus to tune out the dreary arrogance of the biologist.

By three that afternoon, with only a couple of comfort stops, they had found their UFO harbor. As was to be expected, it looked just like any number of small New England river towns in the sun of an autumn day.

Henry remembered that his informant had said that there was a woman at the local newspaper who had become an authority on the UFO and the creature sightings that had been made in the area over the past twenty years. He could not remember her name, but they ventured that she would not be hard to identify to what appeared to be a four-or-five-staff-member newspaper.

When Henry and Ben inquired at the newspaper office for the local UFO expert, the jolly, round-faced woman in her fifties who stood facing them readily admitted that she was the one who fit that description. Her name was Mary Higgins, and being a widow with a very limited social life, she unhesitatingly accepted their invitation to dinner in exchange for her guiding them to one of the more favored UFO-spotting sites.

Mrs. Higgins seemed only mildly impressed by their academic and professional credentials. She had, within the prior four months, brought two astronomers, five magazine writers, an Air Force officer, a documentary filmmaker, and an author of books on the paranormal to the same site to which she would guide them that evening.

Mary Higgins proved to be a delightful raconteur over dinner at the charming riverfront restaurant. She told them that the phenomenon often left scorched circles in the farmers' fields. Some farmers claimed that the UFOs appeared with such regularity over their meadows that they could set their watches by them.

At least half a dozen men and women claimed to have been taken on board the craft, and they all described the UFOnauts as being no more than five feet tall with large heads, big eyes with catlike pupils, hardly any noses to speak of, just a couple of slits for mouths, and pointed ears.

No, she answered Phil Reisman's jibe, they were not green-skinned, but they had been wearing green-colored, one-piece jumpsuits.

Each time Reisman spoke, Mrs. Higgins looked at him with the thinly veiled disgust one reserves for someone who repeatedly breaks wind at a dinner party.

All in all, the little New England river town and its surrounding environs seemed like a perfectly mixed cauldron of continually bubbling paranormal phenomena. For at least the last twenty years—and before that if the old-timers could be believed—there had been regular manifestations of UFOs, UFOnauts, Big Foot, Cat People, Giant Birdmen, ghosts, phantoms, and poltergeists. Grimly, she said in addition to the bizarre parade of creatures and celestial visitors, there had been a number of strange, unexplained disturbances.

Mrs. Higgins favored the theory that she lived in what some physical researchers termed a "window area," an aperature between dimensions of reality, so to speak. A place where, in what seemed to be cyclical patterns, mysterious phenomena continued to appear, then disappear. More aware intelligences, such as the UFOnauts, made use of such window areas to enter and to leave our Space-Time continuum.

Philip Reisman stated his opinion that it all sounded dangerously akin to madness to his way of thinking, and at that moment, in what may have been the purest of coincidences or a remarkable demonstration of mind over matter on the part of Mrs. Higgins, the waiter lost his footing and spilled an entire pitcher of ice water over Reisman's head. Whatever the cause of his dousing, the event was to serve as an omen of Reisman's baptism into a world he had denied could ever exist.

That night at the very stroke of twelve, as beautifully choreographed as if George Pal, Ray Harryhausen, Willis O'Brien, Douglas Trumbull, or any other of the great Hollywood special-effects masters were producing live-action theater, a glowing UFO appeared above the clump of trees before which Chiang had parked his Volvo.

Lazarus felt fully alive for the first time in his life. Chiang was chortling with excitement. Mary Higgins was staring smugly at Philip Reisman, who was saying absolutely nothing, who seemed totally transfixed by the tableau before him.

The Volvo could not contain them. Lazarus flung open the door as if he were his Biblical namesake throwing back the stone before his tomb. Chiang was already racing across the open meadow that lay before the grove in which the UFO appeared to have settled.

"Don't rush it, boys," Mary Higgins warned them. "Don't get too close. Give it a minute."

Reisman shouted at them to come back, to be careful.

When they were about halfway across the meadow, two balls of greenish light moved out from the grove and came toward Chiang and Lazarus. The two physicists slowed their pace and looked curiously at the lights hovering above them.

Mrs. Higgins had stepped out of the car, and she was yelling at them that they were being monitored. Chiang and Lazarus felt that she might be correct.

And as they stood there, not wanting to offend or to transgress any rules they could not hope to comprehend, they heard the crushing footsteps of unseen entities moving in the grove ahead of them. To their right, they heard what seemed to be heavy breathing. To their left, the mumble of hollow, alien voices.

Chiang lifted his arms and shouted into the darkness that he was a man of goodwill and peace. Motivated by his friend's example, Lazarus did the same.

At that moment, the harsh, blaring, horribly discordant sound of the car horn shattered the almost reverential attitude of the two scientists toward the promise that lay beyond them in the grove of trees. The sound of the horn became the shriek of a frightened, demented beast, and it seemed to echo around them in a hundred variations of disharmony.

From the very first note of the metallic scream, every aspect of the UFO manifestation seemed to shrink back, as if the footsteps, the lights, the breathing, the voices were but multiple probings of a single entity—an entity that had now begun to retreat, to withdraw, like a wild thing startled by the blare of a hunter's trumpet.

In the matter of a very few seconds, all facets of the phenomena had seemingly been pulled back to the grove, and Chiang and Lazarus stood in the center of the meadow in anguish, as the UFO shot up into the night sky at a rate of speed that they could not comprehend in terms of the science which they understood. They felt alone, disappointed, like two small children who had only caught a glimpse of Santa's boot as the giftladen elf disappeared up the chimney.

When they returned to the Volvo, they demanded to know why Dr. Reisman had pressed on the horn. His reply was barely distinguishable through his frightened, chattering teeth, but it had something to do with saving them from being taken into a spaceship and chopped up for food.

Mrs. Higgins' face in the light from the headlamps bore an expression composed of nearly equal parts of contempt and pity for the biologist.

"It's scared away now," she told Chiang and Lazarus. "You might just as well call it a night."

They drove Mary Higgins back into town and thanked her for her graciousness and her tolerance.

When they went in search of a motel that might still be open, Philip Reisman insisted that they return at once to Boston. Lazarus and Chiang acquiesced, since another day spent with the man would have been intolerable to both of them.

They were not five miles out of town when Reisman, who was sitting in the backseat, began to shout that they were being followed by two glowing green lights.

When Chiang glanced in the rearview mirror, he was excited to see that Reisman was correct.

Lazarus clutched his friend's shoulder and together, almost as one, they uttered a shared wish that they might have another opportunity for interaction with the UFO occupants.

But then the lights whooshed by them, one on either side, and vanished into the darkness.

By the time Chiang and Lazarus dropped Reisman off at his apartment, the man was nearly hysterical. He had cowered in a corner of the backseat most of the way home, his teeth chattering, his eyes weeping. He had shouted out a dozen times at imagined monsters at the side of the highway.

When they walked into Chiang's apartment thirty minutes later, the telephone was ringing.

It was Reisman, babbling into the receiver about something pounding on his walls.

Ben was about to tell him to take some tranquilizers and to go to sleep when a remarkable thing occurred. A mysterious pounding began on the walls of his own apartment.

At this point, Reisman screamed that a dark, hooded figure had appeared in a corner of his bedroom.

Almost as soon as Chiang repeated for Lazarus' benefit what the man had said, the two of them were gasping at the materialization of a dark, hooded figure in a corner of Ben's living room.

Before either of them could assimilate that phenomenon, the radio unit in the stereo console clicked on, and some unseen agency moved the dial from station to station. Three books were made airborne from the shelf where they had rested. The refrigerator door popped open. All the water faucets in the kitchen and the bathroom were turned to full stream.

The weird, pointless manifestations disrupted both apartments until dawn, about two hours after they had begun.

"We had undergone quite an initiation that night," Henry Lazarus told me later. "And the phenomena continued, even at long distance. I would be in Houston talking to Ben back east in Boston, and he would say, 'Hey, there's that dark hooded figure standing in the corner again,' and, son of a gun, if I wouldn't see a similar figure standing inside my closet door or over in a corner of my bedroom."

Chiang pushed his chair back from the table around which we had been drinking coffee late into the night. "Well, what we theorize occurred is that we somehow activated a reflexive response from a concentration of the X-Force in that community."

"I would say," Lazarus speculated, "that the negative factor was Reisman's fear and resultant hysteria. His emotional reaction to the phenomenon overrode our scientific curiosity."

Henry Lazarus continued the speculation: "We feel that there had been a *genuine* UFO landing near that village at some undetermined time in the past. It was quite likely witnessed by one or more townspeople. This incident became so important to the psyches of the men and women in that rather remote area that their collective energy began to affect the X-Force in such a way that *a phantom was created by the conduit of their group mind*.

"The more energy they invested in the archetype of the UFO experience, the more solid and material it became.

"The more material it became, the more people who witnessed it coming into being, the stronger the phantom of the real UFO experience became."

"There is, we have discovered, a reflexive, imitative aspect of the X-Force," Chiang added. "Again, that is why the manipulator of the Unknown Energy must always strive for balance. If you are at the level of awareness that envisions monsters, you may quite likely fashion them—if your belief is strong enough to affect the X-Force that is all around you."

*Then had it been Reisman's fearful response that had triggered certain negative patterns into which the X-Force could flow and express itself?*

"Yes," Lazarus agreed. "Just remember that with the Unknown Energy, the pattern is everything. Just as with the Hieronymous machine the molecular pattern captured on film emulsion can stand for a man, a woman, or an orchard as they actually are. The symbol becomes the object."

*So once Reisman had become "spooked," he set a whole ghostly repertoire into action—the poundings on the wall, the hooded figures, the poltergeistic activity.*

"That's right," Chiang told me. "And he transmitted these images to us according to the same law of patterns which exists in the X-Force. That is why we must seek to make ourselves pure sending and receiving sets for the energy. We must not permit ourselves to become negative."

*What had happened to Dr. Reisman, the cynical biologist who had his perimeters of reality so broadly stretched for him?*

"I regret to say," Chiang sighed deeply, "that Philip Reisman's life became a tragic comedy. A rigidly closed mind did not serve him well. It is best to be at least *somewhat* open to all aspects of existence, so that when you come face to face with something that has not previously been a part of your reality, you can deal with it without shattering into mental and emotional fragments.

"Dr. Reisman had to resign his post with the university. He became a 'born again' Christian and walked the streets of Boston distributing fundamental Christian literature. The last we heard of him, he was living in a commune in Maine, attempting to chant the nature spirits into helping him grow giant vegetables."

Bill Fogarty began by telling me that he had seen a UFO in April of 1972, when he had been twenty years old. He had been a college junior at the University of Indiana at South

Bend, a member of an informal group that got together once a week to discuss politics, philosophy, art, poetry, and women.

One night someone had brought up the topic of UFOs—and that very evening, driving back to their respective apartments, five of their number claimed to have witnessed a low UFO overflight.

Fogarty assured me that each of the five—and he had been one of them—were all college students, physically fit, nondrinkers, nondopers, and two of them were Viet Nam combat veterans. Each of them prided himself on maintaining a cool, analytical approach to all aspects of life, especially toward anything that smacked of the occult or the bizarre. And yet each of them swore that he had seen what was unmistakably an object in the sky that he could not identify as a conventional aircraft, an ordinary celestial manifestation, a weather balloon, a bird, or anything known that could have been flying above them.

Four nights later, two of the five had seen another UFO. Then, on the next evening, Fogarty and the other two saw a brightly glowing object overhead as they returned around one o'clock from a movie.

The five decided to form a splinter group in order to discuss the UFO phenomenon. They were well aware that the main group of culture vultures would mock them for their flying saucer experiences and make light of the entire subject, so they would head for an all-night pancake house to compare notes and thoughts on their subjective response while undergoing the experience of encountering what appeared to be an unknown phenomenon.

Fogarty said that it had not been long before the five of them had a group sighting, and from that evening on they had taken to nightly skywatches.

"We all witnessed UFOs cavorting in the midnight sky," Fogarty said. "On one occasion I stood within ten feet of two nocturnal lights hovering silently in midair. Later, we heard rappings in the dark, hollow voices, heavy breathing, and the crushing footsteps of unseen entities.

"Strangely enough," Fogarty said, smiling, "we were able to maintain our cool toward all the phenomena occurring around us. Maybe we got to thinking that we had been chosen for some special kind of interaction. Perhaps, secretly, we were beginning to view ourselves as masters of two worlds. I mean, we were all Dean's List students, all athletic young men, normally balanced emotionally, mentally, sexually. I guess we felt that modern Renaissance men such as ourselves could deal rationally with such phenomena and stay in control of the situation."

But then, Fogarty went on, the manifestations had become violent. They had swept through one of the group's home one night, pounding on the walls, yanking furiously at the bedposts, striking the startled young man in the face, terrorizing his entire family. Some of the group were followed by unmarked automobiles that seemed a bizarre mixture of styles and models—phantom automobiles, if you will.

Within the next few months, the number of harrowing incidents had increased and had expanded to include strange, dark-clad, nocturnal visitors in the apartments of several of the group members.

Radio and television sets switched on by themselves. Doors opened and closed—although, when tested, they were found to have remained locked. One of the group made the wild claim that he had been teleported one night from his bedroom to the middle of a forest on the outskirts of the city.

"As preposterous as that sounds," Fogarty said, "I'm sure that most of us accepted it as true, since we had all undergone some incredible experiences. We had all lost our sense of perspective. I began sleeping with the light on and a .38 Special under my pillow. Another of my friends invested heavily in weapons and began running with a group that offered sacrifices to Odin. A third was 'born again' into fundamental Christianity. The other two dropped out of college a month before they would have graduated with honors."

*What did he think it had all meant?*

Fogarty considered the question carefully. "I've thought a lot about that. I think the five of us had entered a kind of game, a contest, a challenge, a testing experience. The trouble was, we just don't know all the rules.

"Modern society doesn't prepare us to play those kind of games. Modern society doesn't tell its kids that there is another reality around them. Our educators have ignored the individual mystical experience and the other dimensions that can open up to those who enter altered states of consciousness—whether it be through drugs or through accidentally stumbling into the twilight zones."

*Is humankind involved in some kind of continuing interaction with the "Other"?*

*Is it the same ancient intelligence that continually tests us, or do new teams come to play the reality game with us?*

"I had the feeling," Fogarty recalled, "that my friends and I were dealing with some kind of energy. At first I thought it was something from outer space, some alien world. But I've thought about our experiences a great deal over the past eleven years, and I believe that we had somehow activated some energy that is a part of this planet. I think we might have triggered some kind of archetypal pattern with our minds. Maybe that's what magicians have tried to do since Cro-Magnon days—interact with and control that energy with their minds."

*How had such intelligent, resourceful young men lost control? Why had they ended up paranoid, frightened, or converted?*

"Because we weren't magicians, obviously," Fogarty chuckled. "We had no idea just how deadly serious the game could become. It really is a game for wizards, not for smart-ass college students who believe their brilliant intellects and their physics books can provide an answer for everything."

Jim Hunter's father had been a senior sales representative for an import company based in the South Pacific. The company was always shifting the Hunters around, but from March of 1964 to May of 1968, they had lived in New Zealand.

Shortly after he had turned seventeen on March 12, 1967, Hunter had gone on holiday at the beach near the little New Zealand ocean town of Kawhai and had been swimming around a section of shoreline that was not usually penetrated by tourists. It was here that he found a flat, smooth metallic object under a tidal rock.

The object was oval-shaped, smooth, rounded at the edges, and engraved with peculiar symbols. It weighed about one pound, and when he found it, it had been tightly wedged between two tide-level boulders that were only exposed at low tide. The object looked very old. Algae and other sea deposits encrusted it.

When such objects are found in New Zealand, they are most often taken for Maori relics, which are in high demand. Hunter's father immediately advised him to take it to a knowledgeable Maori to have it examined.

Two weeks went by, during which time the object passed from hand to hand among Maoris who were experienced in appraising the relics of their people. At last the consensus was delivered to Hunter: The object did not come from anything or any time in their culture.

A man who represented himself as a journalist for the *New Zealand Herald* claimed that he had heard of the object from a Maori contact, and he asked if he might see it. After a few minutes' examination, he expressed his feelings that the object was made of some kind of bronze alloy, and he asked if he might take it to Auckland for some tests.

Hunter refused his request, for his father had already spoken to a friend at the university in Christchurch about the possibility of having a metallurgical analysis run on the object. Hunter could not recall if such an analysis had ever been made, but he did remember that the curio ended up in a dresser drawer in their home in Te Awamutu, where it was to remain until his father received orders to move to New York City in May of 1968.

"That was when I first discovered that the object was missing," Hunter told me. "I knew very well the drawer in which it had rested for nearly a year, but when I came to pack it for moving, it was not there. It had disappeared."

Chagrined, slightly suspicious of one or two friends who might have envied his find, Hunter had nothing to do but to accept his loss.

As they waited for their flight from Auckland International Airport in May, Hunter was approached by two young Polynesian types, who claimed to be from New Zealand Inland Revenue. They asked him if he were taking anything illegal out of the country, and they were especially interested in learning if he had any relics, art objects, or the like.

Hunter's parents were saying good-bye to friends some distance from him, and since the men acted very professional, he had become intimidated by them. He did his best to explain that he had no relics in his possession, but then the two men insisted that he go with them to a hotel in Auckland to undergo a private baggage check. It was at that point that he had summoned his father.

Hunter's father demanded to see their indentification and asked why they couldn't examine his son's baggage right there in the airport. When their answers didn't make sense, his father had summoned a patrolling constable to intervene. His mere arrival seemed to scare the two away, and they shuffled off without other word. The whole incident had seemed very shady and frightening to Hunter.

That fall, back in the United States, Hunter had enrolled in Columbia University for his freshman year. Shortly after the term had begun, he was approached in his room by a middle-aged Italian art dealer who said that he had heard that Hunter had spent some time in New Zealand and that he was interested in purchasing any relics or curios that Hunter might have brought with him.

Although the alleged art dealer was polite and businesslike, he was annoyingly persistent. In spite of Hunter's repeated denials that he had any such relics to sell him, the man had approached him three times before the winter holidays.

Through correspondence, Hunter had learned that three of his closest friends in New Zealand had been questioned by men who seemed to fit the description of the two who had attempted to search his luggage at the airport. In one instance, the New Zealand police had to be called in to block continued harassment. In another case, a girl's life had been threatened.

According to their letters to him, each of his friends had been questioned about whether or not Hunter had given them anything to keep before he had left New Zealand. They all used words like "spooky," "weird," and "creepy" to describe the men who had talked to them.

In 1970, Hunter had transferred to Stanford University. He had no sooner moved into his apartment and had the telephone installed when he received a call warning him never to return to New Zealand.

During a later call, a woman with a high-pitched voice had informed Hunter that he was being kept under surveillance by a group who felt that he had acted unjustly in the past by not returning things to their proper owners.

In 1972, Hunter had decided to teach high school for a time before he continued with his graduate work. That summer, a few weeks before he was to begin his first job in the Sacramento school system, he was vacationing in San Francisco. Late one night, the telephone rang, and it was a jovial, laughing man, who said that Hunter had acted wisely by not returning to New Zealand.

"You must understand what a quiet life I led as an undergraduate," Hunter said. "Yet at both Columbia and at Stanford I probably received thirty or more telephone calls from anonymous voices advising me not to return to New Zealand or reprimanding me for having taken something that did not belong to me. I didn't wear an armband declaring that I had lived in New Zealand for four years, and I seldom discussed my life there with any but a few of my closest acquaintances. Who could possibly have cared about my having found that metallic slab? And who could possibly have taken such a long-term interest in me because of a casual act committed a few days after my seventeenth birthday?"

About the third day after classes had begun in the suburban community of Sacramento where Hunter had accepted a high school teaching position, a student unknown to him had stopped by his room to say hello. Hunter knew that such an act was hardly unusual, since students will often do this to look over a new teacher. But from the first, the boy acted strangely inquisitive.

Hunter was astonished when the teenager stepped to the blackboard and drew the same design that he had first seen on the mysterious object that he had found in New Zealand. He smiled to Hunter, then asked him if he knew what the symbols meant.

When Hunter pressed him, in turn, for some answers, the boy erased the design, laughed, and said that he was just fooling around, that he didn't mean anything by it.

"I never saw the kid again," Hunter said. "I described him to a couple of the other teachers and to a bunch of students, but no one was able to identify him. I doubt very much if he actually went to the school at all."

*Did he still receive calls about the object?*

"I hadn't been at the university more than four days when someone rang my room and scolded me about taking things that didn't belong to me," Hunter replied. "I came here in the fall of 1976 to begin my doctorate program. I had been awarded a teaching assistantship, and I felt very much together with life. Then that damn telephone call came."

*What exactly did it say?*

"It said that I should never take anything from where I had found it," Hunter recalled. "It said that I should always leave things where they were. That I had no right to act unjustly and to take things away from their proper owners!"

Cynthia of Garland, Texas, told us that in 1966 she was well on her way to receiving her doctoral degree when, during an all-night "bull session," she happened to remark that she thought she had extraterrestrial ancestry. Word soon reached the dean of her academic department, who revealed the information to the Dean of Women.

The next thing that Cynthia knew, she was being told that she would either see a psychiatrist, who had been recommended by the Dean of Women, or she would be expelled from the doctoral program. Disillusioned, Cynthia chose to drop out.

"Right now," she writes, "I am most interested in what you have said about the worldwide awakening of the Star People. I thought I was completely alone until I read *Revelation: The Divine Fire* (Berkley Books, 1981) a year ago . . . I know that I did not find the Star People series by accident."

Cynthia revealed that she had had an aunt in whom, as a child, she could confide her experiences with multidimensional entities, but she lamented that she had since learned that she had to be somewhat cautious in whom she chose to share her insights:

You mentioned in *The Star People* that some have been persecuted because of these beliefs and thoughts. I can vouch for that. There are psychological and physical pressures which are utterly incredible.

I believe that there really are dark, demonic forces which are fighting this work until the bitter end. I do not claim to understand the book of *Revelation* in the *Bible*, but I believe there is a passage to the effect that "Satan rages because he knows his time is short."

# Chapter Ten

## CLOSING THE DOOR ON THE LIMBO SPIRITS

Put on the full armor of God, that you may be able to stand firm against the schemes of the devil.
For our struggle is not against flesh and blood, but against the rulers, against the powers, against the world forces of the darkness, against the spiritual forces of wickedness in the heavenly places.

*Ephesians 6:11, 12.*

Satan may appear to be winning the war because sometimes he wins important battles, but the final outcome is certain. One day he will be defeated and stripped of his powers eternally. God will shatter the powers of darkness.

*Billy Graham*

I learned to control my dreams when I was but a boy. It had happened in one of those childhood nightmares that so many people have—one of those in which you can't run, you can't pull the trigger of the gun, and the monster just keeps getting closer and closer.

Then it was as if I stepped out of the dream and called things to a halt. "Whose dream is this?" I demanded.

145

All the monsters quietly conceded that the dream belonged to me.

"All right," I said, dictating the terms of my dreams, "from now on, when I pull the trigger, the gun fires and you fall dead. Understand? It's just a dream anyway, and you won't really get hurt."

All the monsters had understood, and I had been able to stop, start, continue, and otherwise control my dreams from that night onward.

That is with the exception of a nightmare that I endured in December of 1980. But it seemed almost as if that terrible dream were not mine. It seemed as though it really belonged to someone else, someone else who was somehow projecting images upon my sleeping body's brain.

I had fallen asleep in a certain mood of melancholy, for I had been remembering Christmases past. Nostalgically, I had been recalling memories of so many holiday treks with the children to their grandparents' farm home. I recalled how we had sung folk songs and silly parodies of popular ballads as we had driven in our snug, metallic island. .

As my memory patterns had flashed upon scene after scene from previous holidays, I was saddened by an acute sense of terrible loss. It was not so much that I was now separated in miles from three of my children, with my being in Arizona and their being in Iowa, but that we had become separated by time. The days of their childhood were gone to us forever, except in our memories.

It was somewhere in the midst of such melancholy—and emotional vulnerability—that I fell asleep and began to dream. I was once again driving along an Iowa blacktop, but in the dream, the automobile stalled and would not start.

And when I stepped out from behind the wheel to open the hood, I was suddenly all alone somewhere on an Arizona desert.

It was night, and the moon was bright, and I began to walk in a direction that I felt was north. In spite of the moonlight, I was fearful of stumbling into cactus spines, rattlesnakes, Gila monsters, and prickly pears.

In my dream logic, I had as my destination our daughter Tia's apartment in Flagstaff. I knew there would be help there. I knew that she and her friends would help me get back to my home in Scottsdale.

Then I stood at the side of the highway, waving my arms in a desperate pantomime of pleading for a ride.

A cowboy in a Ford pickup truck slowed down, looked at me, then pulled off the side of the highway in the emergency lane. I ran the short distance that separated me from deliverance from the threats of the desert.

The man's face was windburned and weather-beaten. His old brown Stetson was crinkled and dusty. He narrowed his eyes, taking me in, then he smiled broadly in recognition.

"Hey, ain't you Brad Steiger, the writer?" he asked as he reached over and pushed open the door to allow me entrance.

Somehow, even in my dream, it struck me as peculiar—flattering, but peculiar—that anyone, to say nothing of a cowboy in a pickup truck, would recognize me as an author; but I quickly got in the cab and accepted his offer of a ride.

In response to his question of destination, I told him where I was going. "That's no problem," he said, "I'm goin' to Flagstaff, myself. I'll just swing off Highway 17 over to Sedona and take 89 up to Flag."

I thanked him for his kindness, and as he leaned forward to offer me his hand in a friendly gesture, I suddenly found myself holding the plump fingers of Grandma Anna.

"You know that I always want to help you," she said in her Danish-accented voice.

"Just tell me again where it is you want to go," Grandma Anna said. "And I'll take you there, for..."

"...it's no trouble at all," the cowboy completed the sentence. Grandma Anna's image was no longer before me.

"By the way, Brad," he grinned. "My name is Wes, Wesley J. Tyree. Let's blast off. You like to ride, don't you?"

There was a slight blur of movement, and Pastor Maynard Jorgenson was driving the cowboy's pickup.

"You've been a very big disappointment to us all, Brad," he said in that sepulchral voice of his.

Pastor Jorgenson's blue eyes were sad as he turned to face me. "You always knew your catechism perfectly, that was why I asked you to take over the church services when I went on vacation that summer. You were only fifteen, but I knew that you would be as conscientious as any visiting pastor. And I heard that you gave splendid sermons. Of course you couldn't perform the sacraments, but you gave good sermons. I knew you would."

I thanked him, wanting to reach out and touch the man of God. It had been his constantly expressed wish that I would enter the seminary and become a pastor in the Lutheran Church.

"Now, you no longer give sermons," the voice was lamenting. "You only confuse the mind with bizarre images. You write books filled with heresies!"

I had to speak in my defense. "But Pastor Jorgenson, I always write of peace, love and higher awareness."

"But do your books lead people to Jesus?" came the accusative query.

"I hope they lead people to Christ consciousness," I said. "I'm just more universal in my writings, Pastor. I'm not denominational, anymore. I want everyone to find the keys to the kingdom of spiritual peace, not just a chosen few."

There was another ripple of energy, and Grandma Dena, tall and regal, had her capable hands on the wheel of the Ford pickup.

"Don't argue with the pastor," she scolded me. "You remember that I warned you that some of those books that you were reading would come back to haunt you one day. I warned you that you should read only the classics, those books which only enrich the brain. I told you not to read those science fiction pulp magazines."

Wesley Tyree was laughing at me through yellow, tobacco-stained teeth. "Pretty damned good likenesses, don't you think?"

"Stop these obscene charades!" I shouted my rage. "Stop defaming the images of those good people. I know what you really are."

Grandma Dena was scolding me again. "You must stop that shouting. A young gentleman does not shout."

"You aren't my grandma!" I screamed. "Appear as you really are, for I know that you are not Wesley J. Tyree, either!"

Welsey Tyree was back at the steering wheel, chuckling softly, pushing the weathered Stetson back from his forehead. "Wow, Brad, you got to be careful what you asks for, boy. You got to think through very carefully what you says. You didn't really want to see me as I really am, do you? You jus' gotta think things through now that you're going to meet ol' Zoltar hisself."

Zoltar, Wesley told me, was the top honcho in the Disciples of Darkness. I braced myself for another metamorphosis. I could not imagine what form would next occupy the driver's seat.

"Oh, no," the cowboy laughed. "I ain't Zoltar. He'll be waiting for yuh in the cave jus' a few more miles down the road. Boy, you gonna have yourself a real night!"

Within the reality of the night terror I felt my knees trembling. My stomach was churning, and nausea enveloped all of my being. I had never been so frightened in my life. I could not even imagine what might lie ahead of me.

And then I found myself crying out within the very center of my essential self. "Aleah," I called to the entity whom I had seen since early childhood and had always regarded as my guide. "You must help me. Tell me what to do."

Wesley seemed oblivious to the shimmering image of the beautiful woman who appeared next to me in the cab. Straw-blonde hair was piled atop her head, and she was dressed in a loose-flowing robe of purple velvet. Her enormous golden eyes and her lovely smile calmed me with emanations of love. Then she was gone, taking with her a large portion of my fear. I felt much more courageous, knowing that an intelligence outside of myself was concerned about me.

"There be the cave." Wesley had braked the pickup and was pointing to a large cave opening that was shielded by pine trees.

"Get out and get goin'," he commanded gruffly. "You don't keep the top dog waitin' for yuh!"

As I approached the cave entrance I was aware of the heady aroma of exotic spices and incense issuing forth to intrigue my nostrils. There was a rhythmic throbbing of drums, the windlike moaning of flutes and oboes, the ringing of tiny bells, the brassy meetings of cymbals, the high-pitched sighing of string instruments.

As I paused in my ascent toward the opening, I heard a lusty chorus of male voices blending in song with a sensual choir of harmonious female voices. The cave entrance no longer appeared dark and foreboding. Flickering, multicolored lights blazoned an irresistible invitation into the night.

As I entered the cave, a beautiful, full-bodied, dark-haired woman in a flowing, diaphanous gown appeared and clutched my right hand. Her green eyes were shadowed with blue paint; her lips were colored a bright red. Her naked breasts swayed seductively under the wispy material, and she wore only the briefest of panties over her pubic region.

"I am Neferu," she said in a voice that was all the ecstatic sighs of women in love melted into one warm, sweet-scented breath. "I am yours if you wish."

As if her words were a cue, I felt my left hand being squeezed by a handsome young man clad only in an abbreviated loincloth. He was a bit less than six feet tall with shoulder-length blonde hair and bright blue eyes. His muscular definition was sharply defined; his stomach was flat; his thighs were powerful.

"I am Mazeru," he said in a deep voice. "I am yours if you wish."

"Or," Neferu lowered her painted eyelids and smiled seductively, "you can have both of us if you like."

I declined to comment on either offer.

"I have business with one who is named Zoltar," I said boldly, feeling Aleah's strength within me. "I understand that he has gone to some pains to bring me here—wherever we are."

"You are in Zoltar's kingdom," Mazeru told me. "Follow us."

"Follow us to the music and dancing," Neferu added. There were tiny bells looped about her ankles, and they rang melodiously as she walked.

When we turned a large bend of the cave, I was astonished to see a vast panorama of marvelous sights. There was a full moon in a star-washed sky which illuminated majestic pyramids thrusting from a flowered plain toward the dome of heaven. Palm trees were everywhere. I caught the scent of a great river before I saw it, its surface glasslike, mirroring the night sky, supporting pleasure craft with lanterns swinging from extended poles.

The city was wondrous, filled with light, throbbing with sounds, bursting with life. My sense of smell was being challenged by dozens of mysteriously appealing aromas. My imagination was being provoked by the music, the singing, the laughter, the fleeting images I glimpsed in the streets and in the shadows. The houses, temples, and other buildings seemed as ancient as civilization's first toddling efforts at creating habitable dwelling places, yet as sophisticated as if they had been fashioned by skilled special-effects experts for some motion picture epic.

"You are seeing Egypt," Mazeru confirmed the question that was swelling in my mind.

"Egypt as it was nearly five thousand of your Earth years ago," Neferu added, leaning the fullness of her body against my side.

"With more than a few of Master Zoltar's whimsical fantasies thrown in for spice," Mazeru admitted with a ripple of laughter. "Come, the Master is waiting."

I felt as though my senses were bombarded to the point where I must surrender to the spell that was being worked upon them. But, I reasoned, this idea of Egypt cannot exist in this cave in Sedona *all* the time. This Kingdom of Zoltar must also be a mental replication of a pattern which certain powerful intelligences were projecting.

*You are correct, my son.*

Aleah was with me. Her voice was a low, rich contralto, speaking to me inside my head.

*Yes, Brad, I am with you, even in the Kingdom of Zoltar. You will have nothing to fear. You will have only to open your mouth, and the correct words will be there for you to use. You will not even have to think them. You will have only to open your mouth and to speak them.*

The music and the laughter were growing louder. I still felt a nervousness, an apprehension, but my terrible fear of meeting Zoltar had been replaced by a detachment that brought with it a kind of tranquility. The knowledge that Aleah was somehow near to advise me had permitted me to balance my emotions, thus clearing my psyche to become a more perfect channel.

We emerged from a darkened alley to an open plaza, brilliantly illuminated by the writhing flames from a dozen fires scattered about the court. Several men and women in bright and colorful costumes were lounging about the perimeters of the plaza on large pillows and cushions.

Against the east wall, a musical ensemble played harp, flute, lute, lyre, and drums as a spirited accompaniment for nine dancing girls. In the center of the entertainment, six male acrobats were forming a human pyramid. Against the west wall, two muscular men were straining shoulder-to-shoulder in a wrestling bout.

The crowd cheered, either for the acrobats or a favored wrestler, at the precise moment Mazeru spoke. The handsome, young Apollo smiled, understanding that I had not heard him.

"There Zoltar awaits you," he repeated when the applause had subsided.

I sighted along the youth's pointing finger and saw that he indicated a canopied tent amidst a group of men and women sprawled langorously on stuffed cushions. Several slaves and servants scurried from one guest to the other with large trays of fruit, nuts, meats, pastries, breads, and wines. Ranked behind the tent, which had been dyed a lustrous, royal purple, were eight large men with spears and swords, standing at strict attention.

Neferu took my hand. "Come," she said in a husky whisper.

I was very much aware of the scent of musk which she exuded from her generous body. The swaying of her hips was a sensual invitation to forget about all else but the glorious exploration of the delights of physical love.

As we approached the purple tent, two guards lifted aside the filmy gauze that draped its front.

"Enter," the burliest one grunted, his eyes glowing red, as if they were coals in a dying campfire.

Zoltar sat in a high-backed wooden chair that had been painted black and trimmed with gold. He wore a simulation of the traditional pharaoh's headdress and a flowing gown of richest purple silk, belted at the waist with links of gold. About his neck was a fine gold chain that supported a dragonlike insignia, which had also been cast in gold.

"Welcome, Brad Steiger." The voice was as smooth as a mirror and reflective of a host who offers nothing but the finest for his guests. "How do you like the small party which I had arranged in your honor?"

The most compelling thing about Zoltar was his eyes—glistening, black marbles that seemed to burn with intense, dark fires. The complexion of his skin was surprisingly light, almost fair, thus accentuating his ebony beard and mustache. The fingers of his slender hands were very long and covered with rings, and they moved and waved as he spoke, as if he were sculpting the words in air at the same time that he was speaking them with his lips.

"I cannot imagine that I am so important in your eyes," I said, very much aware that the two guards had crossed their sinewy arms behind me as they dug the butts of their spears into the ground. Four beautiful women with dark-lidded eyes looked up at me from their places on the cushions surrounding Zoltar's throne.

"May I speak frankly with you, Brad?" Zoltar asked, leaning forward to fix the full power of his black eyes upon me.

"It's the only way to speak at such times as these," I answered.

Zoltar smiled, as if he were indulging a small child. His air of condescension had been perfected over centuries of steady usage. "Frankly, then, I may say that you are no more important to me than an insect I might mash beneath my boot."

I could not suppress a bit of wry laughter. "I knew you couldn't really like me as a person well enough to throw such a magnificent party. After all, we're total strangers."

Zoltar's mouth became grim, his lips flat and narrowed. "Oh, Brad, we're not strangers at all. I've had my eye on you ever since you were an infant."

An icy chill permeated my body as Zoltar spoke of his having observed me throughout my entire lifetime. The entity's black eyes seemed to want to pierce jagged holes in me.

"As I was saying," Zoltar continued, "I deem not *you* important, but the work that you and Francie have accepted for yourselves does very much annoy us."

My question was obligatory, but it seemed part of the drama to ask it: "You don't really expect me to stop it, do you?"

Zoltar brought long fingers to the bridge of his nose. He closed his eyes as if afflicted with a terrible mental burden. "I am the Repositor of Wisdom for the Disciples of Darkness," he said. "For nearly five thousand Earth years we have been the true Lords of the Earth. You will never be able to defeat us. Your only choice is to join us or be destroyed. It is the only choice that has been available to humankind for lo these many centuries."

I frowned my disagreement. "There have been those men and women in every time and in every place who have chosen good rather than evil. There have been men and women with ethics, nobility, responsibility. . . ."

Zoltar snorted in disgust. "And for the most part, they lived miserable existences, plagued by poverty, disease, and disgrace. You have heard it said that virtue is its own reward. That is true. For the only reward for those among humankind who are supposedly virtuous and supposedly capable of charitable acts is the knowledge that they have performed these meaningless actions. Such 'good works' never bring wealth, health, or physical happiness."

Zoltar rose from his chair. He was much taller than I had estimated, well over six feet. He seemed well built, powerful, yet slender of physique, and he moved with graceful, feline quickness and agility.

"Humans who are not *for* us only suffer, and they never accomplish any damage to our cause," Zoltar argued.

"Consider all the names in the historical ranks of the pious," he sneered. "Bring to mind all the saints, the crusaders, the reformers, the martyrs for this and that cause of alleged righteousness. What lasting effect did any of their deeds of misdirected courage gain them or the humanity which they served so heroically, but so futilely? Reckon in your consciousness all those who died on crosses, who suffered hideous tortures, who faced beasts in arenas, who fought to the last man for their gods and their definition of goodness. Did the death of any of them or all of them make even the slightest difference in conditions on Earth? Did the sacrifice of any one of them or all of them cease the acts of murder, rape, war, torture, mayhem, from ever occurring again?"

"The Earth plane is a place of polarities," I heard my voice answer Zoltar's charge.

*Somehow, by some process unknown to me, Aleah was speaking through me!*

"The Earth plane is a place of learning experiences. If it were for each person to live but once and then to be judged, the situation you described would truly be one of great despair. But the message of all the great saints and saviors, all the inspired holy people and sages of all times is that the Soul, the Essential Self, which resides within each physical expression of humanity, is eternal. And, even more than its eternality, it has the capacity to evolutionize, to progress higher and higher until it once again becomes one with the Source of All That Is."

Zoltar cocked his head, narrowed his eyes menacingly, and lowered his face within inches of my own. "So with the knowledge that your Soul is eternally glowing within your breast, you are able to stand here before me and proclaim that you are not afraid of physical death. Is that true?"

"I do not fear death," I said, my eyes meeting the black

orbs of Zoltar, "but I have certain things which I must do to complete my mission on Earth. You needn't expect any act of martyrdom from me."

Zoltar straightened and shook his head in protestation of the very thought. "I would not expect such stupidity from you, Steiger. I know that you are a practical, sensible, realistic man. Just forget this silly business of your spiritual quest, and you'll be free to blunder through life as you see fit."

"I see fit to continue to work with Francie as a light bearer," I replied, annoyed that my knees had begun to tremble. It was difficult not to feel at least some fear when surrounded by so many fearful forms, even if one level of my consciousness knew—or hoped—that this was all a dream.

Zoltar made a growling sound like that of an angry wolf. "You fool!" He paced about the tent, paused to kick one of the women in his frustration, seemed to take some small pleasure in her cries of pain.

"Why," Zoltar demanded, leveling a long, bejeweled forefinger at my nose, "must you be so stupid? You have already proclaimed that you are not some whimpering martyr. And in spite of your quaint little speech about the Soul being eternal, you know that we are the Lords of the Earth. You can't tell me that you are one of those brainless apes who believes that he shall receive his reward in some milk and honey afterlife. You must be intelligent enough to realize that the only meaningful rewards for one's actions are physical and tangible in the here-and-now."

"What is *your* 'here-and-now'?" I questioned, indicating the illusion of ancient Egypt around us.

"This is Egypt as it was after we rose to power through our mastery of magical energies," Zoltar said smugly. "Don't you like it?"

"But how tangible and physical is it?" I challenged him.

"Real enough for me to summon Besku, the captain of my guards, and command him to carve out your heart!" Zoltar threatened.

"I doubt it," I was blunt in stating my skepticism. "I think that you exist in some other frequency of existence, some other level of reality. I do not question that you and your spooks can influence us on the material level, but I think you have to use one of us if you want any physical acts performed."

"All right," Zoltar laughed, caught in his bluff, "but we

have the best of both worlds that way. You can have the best, too, Steiger. Just forget about writing your books about higher states of consciousness."

"You do not have the best of two worlds." I knew the words were Aleah's coming from my mouth. "You have no world at all. You are master only of an illusion trapped between dimensions. You cannot offer anyone anything of lasting value. The treasures with which you tempt will all turn one day to rust, to dust, to mold, to decay."

Zoltar's black eyes were steaming with rage. His long fingers clenched themselves into fists, and I thought for one fearful moment that he would strike me down. Then I realized that neither Zoltar nor all of his minions could do me physical harm. That, too, was impossible for them to accomplish.

"You have never been anything more than a moderately talented deceiver," Aleah thundered at Zoltar through my agency. "That was why you were banished from the temples where the Star Gods' initiates were teaching the techniques for controlling the Earth Force. You wished only to master the Force for materialistic gain."

"But master it I did!" Zoltar roared his answer to the accusation. "And thousands followed me and my disciples."

"You sought to mimic the Star Gods," Aleah continued; "you, too, sought to rise to a higher dimension. But your negativity caused you to fail. You could only rise as high as this Limbo world."

"But see how good it is," Zoltar snapped defensively. "Where have you seen lovelier women, more handsome men, lustier cities, nights filled with more merriment?"

"What are these transient delights of the flesh compared to one heartbeat of Unity with All That Is!"

"Blasphemer!" Zoltar shouted, covering his ears beneath the fold of the headdress, clamping his ring-studded fingers against his skull. "Don't speak of such things here!"

"You only have elevation by perspective," Aleah pressed on through my channel. "You can be high only if you can keep humankind low. That is why you must seek continually to possess the bodies of Animal Man and cause him to commit acts that poison the spirit. The most important thing to you is that you keep humankind on a lower, physical, animal-level so that you will always have an earthly kingdom in which to manifest and humans to subjugate."

"We are the true Lords of the Earth!"

"But of no higher place may you ever be lords," I mouthed Aleah's malediction. "Humankind has the potential to rise to a dimension that is their birthright due to their cosmic heritage. You have forsaken your Starseeded inheritance and exchanged it for a place that can only exist as long as chaotic energy can find a physical realm in which to express itself. You can only be lords if you can manage to keep humankind debased."

Zoltar's laughter was confident. "And that is hardly a challenge! The great masses of humankind are such mindless goats that we shall always be lords of this planet. Our seeds of discord shall always produce quick and productive harvests, especially when I have such devoted husbandmen as these at my command...."

Zoltar waved his hands in the manner of a professional magician. "Behold," he grinned proudly, "my chief disciples from Sumer and Egypt."

There was a murky cloud of smoke wafting about the tent that suddenly became a fierce representation of a hulking brute with mad eyes and a wide mouth made threatening by pointed and broken teeth.

"This is Sebah of the Inner Council," Zoltar introduced the monster. "Sebah was a master of what the squeamish in ancient Egypt called the Black Arts. Throughout the centuries, Sebah has been the great general of all malignant thoughtforms and of those possessing spirits who crave physical bodies with which they might continue to indulge their lusts. Sebah directs them to weak or confused members of humankind who yield their bodies to the invading hosts."

"Demons," I deduced without benefit of Aleah. "You're talking about demons."

Zoltar made a clucking sound and shook his head in disapproval. "That is not an acceptable term here, Steiger."

Another wavering cloud of energy was manifesting into human form.

"Ah," Zoltar said, welcoming the second materialization, "how good it is to see you, Nementu."

Nementu was a tall, muscular, bearded man, whose red-rimmed eyes stared coldly at me from under the rim of a metal helmet. Only Nementu's great arms were bereft of leather and metal pieces of armor. In his right hand he gripped a large sword.

"Nementu the Slaughterer is our pet name for this member of the Council," Zoltar added with an affectionate chuckle. "Those spirits who still hunger for bloody battle flock to the standard of Nementu."

Before Zoltar had completed Nementu's introduction, a third image had expressed itself to the left of the black throne chair. As soon as its form seemed solid, the slender entity had begun making frank sexual overtures to one of the women who lay on the cushions and pillows of the tent.

"Aatenset burns always with the fires of lust," Zoltar shook his head in understanding. "Speak to him of love and tender emotions, and he laughs in your face. Romance is a mockery to Aatenset, a senseless series of rituals that delay the physical release of pure, rutting sex. The spirits who follow Aatenset have the greatest of opportunities to keep humankind at the animal level, for what need is stronger felt within men and women than the urge to procreate? There is hardly any challenge, for the survival instinct aids in keeping sexual expression a compulsion."

"Ah, Zoltar," came a voice that was as expressive as the sound of golden coins falling against one another in a purse, "there is one lust that equals that of sex, and that is the one for gold."

In a bright, golden flash, a beautiful woman with golden blonde hair, golden eyes, and soft golden skin appeared in a tent. I could not help thinking of her as a counterfeit of Aleah. There seemed little question that this entity utilized the X-Force to manifest gold in order to feed an insatiable greed for wealth.

"Samu, as always, wins her point simply by making an appearance," Zoltar conceded. "Who can dispute the powerful hold of money upon humankind, eh?"

Within a matter of moments, I had been introduced to ten of Zoltar's chief disciples, who, together with their master, made up the original Inner Council of the Disciples of Darkness. Before him now, in addition to Sebah, Nementu, Aatenset, and Samu, stood Hetemna the Destroyer, Satem the Assassin, Zefta the Thief, Ketutsen the Torturer, Zeptet the Bestial, and Amenhi of the Flashing Knives.

"Impressive, aren't they?" Zoltar asked, as if he expected me either to applaud or to fall to my knees in obeisance. "And behind each of these, my trusted generals, are grouped countless thousands of spirits who have been drawn here to Limbo.

And the greater the population of humankind, dear Brad, the greater the fruits of our harvest. Join us, for there is no way that you can prevail against us."

I needed no time at all in which to make my decision. "Zoltar, those men and women who have responded to the seed within them have always prevailed against you. Throughout history there have been those who have chosen to become as spiritual warriors and resist your legions."

"And of what good has their resistance been?" Zoltar demanded. "Wars, crimes, promiscuity, drug abuse, pornography! Tell me, are these things increasing or decreasing on Earth today?"

"For every power-hungry statesman preaching war, there is a diplomat negotiating peace," I said, feeling the energy of Aleah at my side. "For every angry criminal attacking society, there is a policeman defending it. For every man or woman who yields to the hungers of the flesh, there is one who is practicing discipline and morality. For every cruel pusher of drugs in the streets, there is a devoted doctor or nurse in the rehabilitation centers helping those who have abused recreational drugs to start the road back to life. For every man or woman who exploits the sex drive through debased and pornographic depictions of love, there are the sincere teachers, concerned clergy, and loving parents who are showing youth a balanced and nonexploitative man-woman relationship.

"Sure, Zoltar," I shrugged in a detached manner. "You win the battles. All over the world, every day—you are winning the battles. But mark this well, and I sense that you already know it, we are going to win the war!"

Zoltar's answer was calm, confident. "In spite of the conserted efforts of those humans who are foolishly choosing to evolve spiritually, I would say that there will be no contest. Earth will always be ours. Humankind will always provide us with their animal bodies for our pleasures.

"We here in Limbo exist on a finer frequency than yours. Of ourselves, we can only influence, misdirect, confuse, and possess you into performing our desires. But your miniscule intellects and your physical weaknesses provide us with few challenges.

"We have invited you to join us, for we acknowledge your skills in communication," Zoltar said. "We know that you could be of great service to us. It would be so much easier for you if you chose to defect to our cause. But should you not choose to do so, we will simply permit those humans already in our camp to subvert your work."

I felt despair. It often seemed to me as though the Lightworkers were outnumbered by thousands to one.

"Join us," Zoltar was smiling confidently. "We know what is best for the good of your country, the good of your world, and the good of your universe. We know what is best for the good and the gaining of all humans on the material plane."

From my period of piety, when I used to read my Bible each night before falling asleep, a passage came to my lips: "But what shall it profit a man if he gain the whole world but lose his own soul?"

Zoltar frowned in extreme distaste, as if I had committed an unpardonable breach of social etiquette. "Have it your way, Brad Steiger. It matters little to us. We know that you and your insufferably stubborn kind can never prevail against us."

I found myself wondering if Zoltar were correct. Could it be that we had no allies on Earth?

*Only those with awareness of the spirit*, Aleah's voice came to me. *Only those who nurture the seed within and establish contact with the Source without.*

Zoltar's smug features were suddenly replaced by the glowing face of my bedside clock as I opened my eyes to wakefulness. I was thankful that Francie was still up, working on the Star People mail in her office. Somewhat desperately, I interrupted her labors for some information about the Limbo Spirits.

Francie had been well aware of my general skepticism toward the possible existence of malignant entities, so she began her explanation rather cautiously.

"Brad," she told me, "you must be aware of the fact that there truly do exist lower plane spirits which continually seek to possess the bodies of Animal Man. They seek always to control subjects whom they might subjugate. But understand, too, that the awareness that comes with spiritual enlightenment—the eternality of the Soul, the power of unconditional love, the magic of channeling planetary and spiritual energies—totally renders the lower spirits powerless."

I told her the details of my dream. The Limbo Spirits had

seemed very powerful in the bizarre inner drama that I had just experienced.

"They are not omniscient," Francie explained. "They do have their limitations. They cannot, for example, truly see the future. But they do have access to more precise probabilities than do mortals.

"They can be deceived—at least for a time. They can be misdirected.

"And—this is important for you to understand—they cannot achieve power over a human unless they are somehow invited into the person's private space—or unless they are attracted to an aura by that person's negative thoughts and actions."

*Were the Limbo Spirits what humankind has called "demons"?*

Francie nodded, clicking off her desk lamp and leaning back in her chair. "They are parasites of the Soul. They feed of negativity. They grow fat and bold on it, and they are attracted to any human who emanates negative thoughts or who commits negative actions. The Limbo Spirits crave to continue to experience the excesses of the flesh which they so enjoyed when they were in human bodies. For this reason, they are always seeking physical shells to possess in order to perpetuate their lusts."

I stopped my nervous pacing and sat down on the sofa next to Francie's desk. "Remember," she continued, "men and women are especially susceptible to such spirit invasion when they are exploiting one another sexually, when they are drunk on alcohol, when they are drugging themselves into an altered state of consciousness wherein their normal boundaries of control have been removed."

Most of all, Francie emphasized, the Limbo Spirits wished humankind to remain ignorant of its starseeded heritage. They wanted humankind to remain unaware of its potential of reaching beyond itself. It was the master plan of the Limbo Spirits to keep humankind forever incapable of linking up with higher intelligences.

*Why couldn't our spiritual guides intercede for us? Why couldn't they combat the Limbo Spirits for us?*

"Our guides cannot physically interfere with any actions which take place on this plane of existence," Francie explained.

"That may seem unfair, and such a state of affairs does most certainly impede the progress of our own goals, but the laws do exist—and it is impossible to violate them. Our guides can counsel us, warn us, suggest courses of action, but there is no possible way that they can interact with us or with our adversaries on the physical level."

What was important for us to understand, Francie stressed, was that any physical act of good that must be accomplished on Earth must be performed by an Earthling in whom existed the spiritual seed. The Light Beings could only guide us.

*If we cannot rely on our guides for physical protection, how might we protect ourselves?*

Based upon her years of communication with her guide, Kihief, Francie presented me with the following guideline which will assist us in thwarting the Limbo Spirits:

Never enter meditation with the sole thought of attaining personal satisfaction or ego aggrandizement. With such selfish motivation, you run the risk of becoming easily affected by those spirits who have become entrapped in a hellish domain of their own making, a limbo world of discordant vibrations.

Whenever you explore the psychic world through any of the "occult arts," such as astrology, ouija boards, Tarot cards, and so forth, practice a firm sort of mind control so that you will interact only with those entities in the realm of the most loving, harmonious vibrations.

When seeking contact with higher intelligences, remember always that our physical reality is closer to the realm of the lower, more chaotic, frequencies than it is to the dimension of the most harmonious. Because we exist in a material world, the efforts of humankind will always be more of the lower vibratory realm than of the higher planes. We are, therefore, continuously engulfed with the lower dimensions, and we find it much easier to make contact with them.

When you are in communication with an enlightened being from the higher spiritual worlds, you will feel yourself bathed in a wondrous expression of love. You will experience an unconditional love for all living things. You will know no fear from such an encounter.

If you should experience contact with a being from the chaotic realm, you will feel at once a prickling sensation that will seem to crawl over your entire body. You will instantly be filled with doubt, which will soon become a mounting terror or a distinct sensation of unease—depending upon the strength of the discordant vibrations emanating from the spirit.

If you should ever establish such a contact with such a chaotic being, a Limbo Spirit, utter prayers and blessings of love. Fill your entire essence with unconditional love for all living things—including the communicating spirit.

Then, image in your mind that you are closing a door, a great, heavy door, shutting off that particular contact and blocking it from you. Do not speak to it or listen to it again. Shut it off from your psyche, and it will venture forth to find another who will receive it.

In the realm of the discordant, all manner of spirits may be found. Some are merely bewildered, uncertain as to what occurred to them when their moment of physical death came. Others may be furious, filled with an anger beyond reason for having been drawn to the chaotic realm of their own creation.

The angry spirits will continue their discordant ways beyond physical death, and they will often attempt to influence the minds, and thereby the lives, of those who will receive them. These spirits must be cast out from your mind and your life.

In order to prevent contact with the entrapped entities of Limbo, you must practice loving all living things unconditionally; and you must seek to elevate the consciousness of all humankind by your actions.

When you vibrate with the highest form of love, when your purpose is that of the angels, you will make contact only with those entities who are in the realm of the highest vibrations. And you will receive meaningful, inspirational, contact with your own angelic beings from the realm of the highest order.

# Chapter Eleven

## COMMUNICATING WITH THE SPIRITUAL GUIDE

> Millions of spiritual creatures walk the earth unseen, both
> when we sleep and when we wake.
>
> *Milton*

Francie and I had just announced that it was time for a break
during one of our Star People Celebrations which we were
conducting in the ballroom of a hotel in a large city in the
South. We had just led those gathered through a series of
altered-states experiences designed to awaken the seed within
their psyches and to inspire them to begin their earthly missions
without further delays. While Francie was resting in our room,
I decided to stretch my legs before our next session began.

As I walked through the lobby, I could not help overhearing
one of the Star People celebrants, an attractive young brunette,
discussing certain concepts of her cosmology with two men,
who were apparently with one of the other conferences that
were meeting in the hotel that weekend. I picked up the pages
of a newspaper that had been discarded on one of the over-
stuffed sofas next to an artificial palm tree. Then, in a classic
bit of subterfuge, I shielded myself behind the editorial pages

so that I might listen to the conversation without being drawn into it.

"And how long do you believe that you have had this ghost of yours?" the younger of the two men asked the brunette, whom we'll call Sarah.

"I call him my guardian angel," Sarah corrected him gently. "He first appeared to me when I was about five. I've heard him talking in my head ever since. That's the best way I can describe it."

The older man chortled a bit condescendingly. "You're too pretty to be crazy, honey. Why do you think an angel came to you? Are you some kind of religious nut?"

His friend waved him silent. "I try to be open to all kinds of experiences," he said. "I know that there is something beyond us, but are there really angels who talk to people inside their heads?"

"Motu came to me because I have a mission to perform," Sarah said, becoming a bit defensive.

"I have work to do, too, miss," scowled the older man. "But I don't have an angel talking to me inside my head. And what kind of name is 'Motu' for an angel, anyway?"

"They don't really have names the way we do," Sarah explained. "They only have vibratory patterns by which we might reach them in meditation."

"You mean," the older man smiled sardonically, "that 'Motu' is only your angel's area code?"

Sarah ignored the cynicism. "Motu and his kind *seem* like angels to us. They might not really be, you know, angel-angels, but they are very high spiritual beings. And they *do* care about us in a loving way."

The younger man opened his arms expansively and smiled up at the ceiling. "I'm glad there's someone or something that cares about us—especially in a loving way," he said. "That's what this old world needs more of—love, sweet love."

The older man had finished lighting his cigar. The dark smoke he blew over his shoulder seemed to match the dark tones of his skepticism. "Why would those angels care about us? We sure as hell are not very damn lovable as a species."

"I think," Sarah paused as if to receive the right words, "it's because we are like their children. It's as if they created us."

The one with the cigar indicated his confusion with an open palm held up like a traffic cop halting a speeding vehicle. "Hold it right there! I've always had trouble with Adam and Eve in the Garden. Don't give me a bunch of angelic Dr. Frankensteins in there, too."

The younger man could see that Sarah had been offended. "Don't mind him," he apologized for his friend's rudeness: "Jerry has never been noted for his debonair manners."

As if betrayed, Jerry sniffed haughtily and turned to walk away. "The girl is crazy," he pronounced over his shoulder by way of judgmental dismissal.

What she was talking about, Sarah spoke now with renewed enthusiasm to the young man, was what people read about in the Bible, in *Genesis*, about the Sons of God and the Daughters of Men coming together and producing giants in the Earth.

"Many men and women today are the direct descendents of those unions," she told him. "I know that I am."

Her now captive audience of one sighed in exaggerated despair. "Well, I guess that leaves me out," he shook his head slowly. "I'm not Jewish."

Sarah's frown indicated her lack of comprehension. "What does that have to do with anything we're talking about?"

The young man thought it was apparent. "Well, don't we get all that Sons of God and Daughters of Men, giants in the Earth business from the Old Testament, the Hebrew tradition?"

Sarah's mouth made a silent "oh" before she clarified things for him. She explained that she was talking about the Star Gods, the Angels, the Star People, and that they were mentioned in every tradition—the Incas, the Mayas, the Amerindians, the Chinese, the Norse, the Greeks, and the Egyptians, as well as from the tribesmen of the hills and deserts of Palestine. We are just more familiar with the legends of some people than others.

It was time for me to be getting back to the elevated stage in the hotel's ballroom so that we might begin the next session. Francie was probably already there, wondering why I wasn't getting the cassettes ready for the group altered-states experience.

The last that I heard as I left Sarah and her inquisitor was a bit of her description of how Motu had taken her out of her body to a place in space where he showed her visions. I hoped that she might utter just the right words to trigger a sympathetic response from her listener, but as I glanced at the indulgent expression on his attractive young features, I was fearful that she was losing him to the materialistic programming that had possessed his psyche for so long.

It is more than a bit difficult in the Technocracy of the 1980s for those of us who communicate with our guides to find patient and tolerant audiences. Regardless of how practical the guidance received may be, regardless of how productive we may be in our society, we must be cautious to whom we confide that we hear the advice of angels or the counsel of spiritual guides. And recently, Julian Jaynes believes that he has identified such "voices of the gods" in his book, *The Origin of Consciousness in the Breakdown of the Bicameral Mind.*

If Jaynes is correct, humankind existed without consciousness for thousands of centuries, functioning antlike in colonies and being directed by hallucinatory voices which survive today in schizophrenics. These inner voices were assumed by primitive humankind to be divine, and they had given rise to all religions.

Even though humans developed language around 100,000 B.C., according to Jaynes they had no inner existence (consciousness) until around 10,000 B.C. In those intervening years, men and women moved about as sleepwalkers, functional, but not aware. Like rats set loose in a maze, they could solve rudimentary problems, but they possessed no abilities of introspection, imagination, or projection to past or to future. Without consciousness, they were guided primarily by habit.

But new situations would produce stress and the need for new forms of action, thus necessitating the creation of the inner voices as aids in problem solving. Such interior guidance, the commingled side effects of language and primitive self-assertion, permitted humans to remain at survival tasks for longer periods of time.

Eventually, the human brain evolved to integrate the voices. Humans became "bicameral," utilizing the left side of the brain for speech, the right hemisphere for the production of the interior dictator.

And as the brain evolved, so did the society which it produced. By about 1000 B.C., Jaynes theorizes, human culture had grown too complicated to be controlled by the simple commands of the inner voices. Certainly the written word did a great deal to undermine the godlike authority of the voices, although certain of the last pronouncements of the gods which were written down may have become the beginning of law.

In Jaynes' view, then, the "voices of the gods" are subdued in modern man because we are firmly fixed in a conscious world. The voices of the right side of the brain still do break through, as in the cases of such figures as Joan of Arc, contemporary mystics, drug users, and schizophrenics. It is clear to Jaynes that even though the voices could be awakened within certain special individuals, to do so would be to create a person no more able to function in the modern world than can a schizophrenic.

But perhaps we are speaking of vastly different matters. Janyes may offer us some provocative insights into an aspect of humankind's evolution as a social creature. His general thesis may have valid elements contained within the structure of his academic argument.

I, however, am speaking of guidance from Higher Intelligences—entities who appear to be quite separate from the men and women who receive their wisdom and guidance. This faculty of communicating with the guide is hardly limited to "certain special individuals" who are henceforth unable to function in the modern world.

The voluminous mail which we have received from readers of the Star People series has demonstrated unequivocally that thousands of contemporary men and women are unashamedly interacting with their spiritual guides. What is more, these men and women come from every conceivable walk of life. We have heard from scientists, educators, military officers, concert pianists, members of the clergy, law enforcement personnel, journalists, medical doctors and nurses, psychiatrists, as well as truck drivers, cowboys, stevedores, farmers, housewives, students, and commercial fishermen—all of whom profit materially and spiritually from contact with a source of strength and guidance external to themselves.

Following are just a few of the hundreds of inspirational stories which we received from those men and women who have experienced contact with multidimensional entities, who dramatically indicated that they truly cared about their spiritual seedlings on Earth.

Charla of Ashtabula, Ohio, was five years old, alone in her bedroom, when she heard someone call her by her first name. She turned around to see a tall, slender woman, dressed in a long, white gown with flowing bell sleeves. At the waist of the gown was a "glittery pyramid shape." Her shoulder-length hair was silver white. Her skin was very pale, and she had large, light blue eyes.

Charla opened her mouth to speak, but no sound could issue forth.

The beautiful woman smiled and opened her arms to me. In my mind I heard her say, "I am pleased with you, Daughter."

I thought, "You're not my mother. Who are you?"

She laughed and said, "In time you will know me. I am all you are, have been, and will become."

I turned to call my mother, but for some reason turned back to see the woman fade away before my eyes. As she faded, she said, "Don't forget me. Always remember me."

In Charla's case, the female was later replaced by a male of similar description—tall, slender, silver haired, pale-skinned, light blue eyes.

Sometimes he comes to me in dreams or by voice only. He tells me things that are about to happen to myself, family, and friends. He sometimes warns me of things before they happen. I'm always glad that I listen to him.

Phyllis of Cedar Falls, Iowa, still maintains contact with the robed mentor who saved her life when she was five years old.

Mother called for me to return home, and I ran out into the street, not noticing the traffic. Too late I saw the oncoming truck and, trying to stop, I fell into its path. My friend in his white robe pulled me away just in time. He told me that it was not my time yet.

Bruce is a husky ambulance attendant from Louisiana. Although he is now devoted to serving his fellow members of humankind, he went through a period of his life when he withdrew from participation in the flow of society.

Lynda, a spirit being with brown eyes and dark brown hair, was my only true friend throughout high school and college. In the first semester of my junior year in college, she directed me to a psychologist whom she said would be able to restore my faith in humanity. After a year of treatment, she left me, saying that she would always be near if I needed her.

Since then, I have had contact with her via mental instruction and out-of-body experiences. On occasion, I have also had visual contact with Lynda and a male, who is about six feet tall with long dark hair and beard and soft, brown eyes. He is dressed in a white robe and has a glowing radiance about him. He emanates love. He told me once that my time was near.

Ann is a bank teller from Grand Rapids, Michigan, who remembers that, at age eight, a voice awakened her during a thunderstorm and told her to get out of bed at once. If she hadn't obeyed, she notes wryly, she would not have been writing her experience to us today: "Because seconds later lightning hit the metal screen above my bed and shot across my pillow."

A few years ago, Ann told us, the voice helped her again.

I was in the woods alone, feeling intense depression. Then a voice came on a wind and said: "God made me what I am."

The effect was a total lifting of my mood—a release, somehow, from fears and stresses.

The first time that William, a secondary school teacher from Highland Park, Illinois, saw his guardian angel, he initially felt fear.

But as he tucked the covers around my shoulders, he radiated love and benign comfort. He then sat on the bed and watched me until I fell asleep. I was aware of his presence on several nights.

Maurice, a social worker in Topeka, Kansas, claims that he has heard a voice that has saved him from danger on several occasions.

This inner voice is a blessing to me. It saved my life twice in Korea.

Once it told me to step back just as a heavy piece of glass fell from a high ceiling. It smashed right at my feet.

The voice has saved me from unpleasant or harmful experiences and guided me to what I later learned were the wisest courses of action.

Linda Jo is an emergency medical technician in Columbiaville, Michigan. She was about eight years of age when she was lying in bed late at night, crying out her unhappiness.

I felt a presence in the room and, turning, I saw a woman whose shape was all in shining white. She was standing by my bed, smiling at me. She did not speak, but she reached down and stroked my hair. The love and the warmth from her caused me to relax and to drift off to sleep.

When Linda Jo was nineteen, she broke through the ice of a lake on a cold day in February. She was alone, and no one could hear her screams for help. The cold water was about to pull her under when . . .

A voice came to me and began giving me instructions on how to get out of the water. I obeyed the instructions and, as exhausted as I was, I managed to get out.

To this day I am warned of danger by my guides. Usually the warnings come in the form of a voice inside my head.

Tom, a writer-producer from St. Petersburg, Florida, was just a child of four, playing on the seashore in south New Jersey, when a wave came over him and dragged him several feet under the surface.

I left my body and watched as my family pulled me from the waters and tried to work life back into my body. My guardian met me and reminded me of the urgency of living in this time period . . . He told me that it was my choice to stay or to return again later. I chose to fulfill my original mission, which I now realize is as a Starseed.

Clarissa, of Vancouver, Washington, is a chiropractic assistant, who experienced a remarkable restructuring of her physical body through the ministrations of her guides.

The experience changed my life! I weighed three hundred pounds. I was fat, ugly, unhappy, unhealthy, and mean.

Someone woke me and told me to go to the living room. I was told to lie on the couch, but I was nervous and began to pace.

After about three to five minutes, some unseen hands gently pushed me down on the couch. I "sensed" seven entities, five male and two female, although I could not see them.

A female at my head reassured me by saying: "It's all right. We are only cleansing you."

It was like they were dragging a fishnet through my body. They took the real "me" about three feet from my physical body, which then felt only about three inches thick. It was as if they were kneading me. When they were finished, it felt as though they opened up my ribs and pushed me back in.

As I said, I never saw them, but I did see some sparkling lights. Later, on two occasions, I saw two hooded figures.

The "cleansing" was obviously highly successful. Clarissa now carries 140 pounds on her five-foot-eight frame, and she sent us an attractive photograph of herself in costume as "Lia, a high priestess from the healing temple."

Patricia L. Mischell is a psychic sensitive who has her own radio show, *The Psychic World*, in Cincinnati, Ohio. As a child of five in her native West Virginia, she awakened to see a man with beautifully slanted eyes and bronze skin sitting on her bed. "You will never be alone," he told her. "I love you." And then he was gone.

She met her guardian again when she was nine. It was as if an electrical current was rushing through her body. Again he assured her that he would always be with her.

During a near-death experience when she was fifteen, Patricia was told that she must go back to the world to help spread the true message of God.

I returned to my body with a purpose. That is when I joined the Sisters of the Poor. But after many days of praying and meditating upon God, I realized that my heart was not content to remain where it was. I asked permission to leave.

I went back into the world, but I decided not to return to school. From that time on, my school was what my guide taught me.

I have not experienced many astral journeys with my guide. I have met with adepts and with visitors from other galaxies. I believe that I have even been taken to a planet where I have lived before in another lifetime.

Each time the guide who came to me as a child is with me. Each time I return from one of these voyages, I know that my very being is different. Each time my Soul wants more and more to help humankind.

Mary of Middletown, Ohio, describes her guide as a man who is tall, thin, and very old. He wears a brown robe with a cowl, much as a Franciscan monk.

Mary goes on to say that her spiritual mentor is rather stern and impersonal, simply instructing, then leaving quickly. Often he dictates such messages as the following:

We are all . . . bonded in Divine Love, striving together toward a common goal—Christ consciousness. Childish yearnings for positions of hierarchy in this attainment are illusions and immaterial in the final analysis. Let the personality lie dormant on the path, and allow the ego to be shaken like a reed until broken: Then the Master's steps may walk, unfettered, across the pure and humble Soul.

When we first met, Francie told me that she was aware of a glowing image of The Blessed Mother standing behind me. Interestingly, just days before we found each other in this lifetime in Saratoga Springs, New York, I had completed the "Return of the Great Mother" chapter in *Gods of Aquarius* (Berkley Books, 1980).

I have always felt especially responsive to the Great Mother vibration. As I have indicated earlier and in other works, the entity that I have perceived to be aiding me in my work is a

statuesque blonde woman with golden eyes whom I know as
Aleah. I believe it to be her voice that prompts me and spurs
me into creativity.

On the other hand, it is a masculine voice that counsels me
as to how best to utilize the concepts which Aleah brings to
me. Time after time, this imageless voice has kept me up all
night, guiding me in refining the most precise presentation of
Aleah's ideas and thoughts.

I hardly think it coincidental that the Greek Muses, those
entities who manifested themselves to inspire artists, poets, and
thinkers, were always depicted as females. And isn't "Neces-
sity" the "mother" of invention?

Francie explains all this very well in *Reflections from an
Angel's Eye* when she speaks of our Souls consisting of the
Feminine-Creative Principle and the Masculine-Guiding Principle. Again, it is the feminine aspect that inspires, the masculine aspect that shapes and refines. And it seems likely that,
from time to time, these facets of our Souls may assume the
archetypal images most suitable and most understandable to
the individual who desires to manifest materially that which he
creates mentally.

The balance of male and female is so essential to any meaningful creative expression that we would urge any business,
any corporate structure, any committee of any kind to be certain
to include a mix of men and women in any brainstorming
session. In our present cultural expression it may still have to
be the males who implement most plans, but they should never
prevent any residue of pride or latent macho mentality to hinder
them from accepting creative input from the females present.

The Feminine-Creative Principle is deeply a part of each of
us, and it must be given its proper due in our lives. The Holy
Spirit is recognized as an expression of the feminine aspect of
the Godhead. God the Father is the basic, organizing and struc-
turing principle in the Universe; but God the Mother is the
creative energy that inspires all formulations required for the
realization of thoughts, words, and deeds.

Elaine Pagels in *The Gnostic Gospels* tells of a newly discovered text from Nag Hammadi, *Trimorphic Protennoia* (Tri-
ple-formed Primal Thought), that celebrates the feminine
principle, the Holy Spirit:

[I] am . . . the Thought that [dwells in] [the light] . . . I move
in every creature . . . I am the Invisible One within the All . . . I

am perception and knowledge, uttering a voice by means of Thought. [I] am the real Voice. I cry out in everyone, and they know that a seed dwells within."

Controversial Roman Catholic priest-author Rev. Andrew Greenley (*The Cardinal Sins*) told religion writer Richard Lessner, in the *Arizona Republic* (May 15, 1982), that the concept of God as a woman had recently seized him and he planned to explore it in a forthcoming novel. Explaining that in Catholic theology Mary reflects the femininity of God, Rev. Greenley said that Catholics needed a more complete awareness of the feminine aspect of God's nature:

> God as woman—now that's a good idea. Our research shows that twenty-five percent of those under thirty have thought of God as a woman. This is an idea whose time has come. This will show up in art and literature and will offend some and fascinate others.

Our good friend Philip K. Dick, author of *Do Androids Dream of Electric Sheep?* (filmed as *Blade Runner*), *The Man in the High Castle, Valis,* and thirty-one other published novels, often told Francie and me of the entity that manifested herself around him in 1974. She was, he said, a "tutelary spirit," possessed of "a transcendentally rational mind."

The voice, which had come to Phil sporadically since his high school days, spoke to him in terse, succinct sentences and communicated most often when he was falling asleep or waking up. He told us that he had to be very quiet and attentive in order to hear the brief messages which she relayed.

The voice identified itself to him as *Ruah,* the Old Testament word for the Spirit of God.

Although Ruah had not spoken to Phil since he completed his book *The Divine Invasion*, he told Francie, in discussing manuscript portions of her *Reflections*, that he had also been shown a vision similar to the one which she describes of the Source and the Divine Plan. He was extremely excited that she had captured the experience so well in "mortal words."

In March of 1974, when his "DNA memory packet exploded," Phil had been instructed in a vision to obtain *Revelation: The Divine Fire*. He did as Ruah instructed and had "a number of missing areas filled in for me." Then it took him five years "to arrive at a place where I will put the concept forth as fiction [*Valis, The Divine Invasion*]."

The week of his transition in March of 1982, I picked up the telephone on two occasions to call Phil. He had spoken of "making a pilgrimage" to compare notes on the Star People research with me and on teaching visions from the Source with Francie, and I wished to finalize plans for his visit.

In each instance, I cradled the telephone just as the electronic impulses had begun their ringing. I felt a definite blockage, a distinct impression that I should not disturb Phil at that time.

It wasn't until three days later that a mutual friend and editor called to tell me that Philip K. Dick, visionary author, mystic, master of the science fiction genre, had left the physical plane.

There are many methods and mechanisms by which the seeker may establish a working contact with a tutelary spirit. Our daughter, Tia, for instance, utilizes the time-honored technique of the tapping table.

I remember very clearly the first time that my son Steve and I accepted an invitation to join Francie and her children Christopher, Tia, Michael and Regina around the "talking" table. We had just finished an evening meal of lacto-ovo-vegetarian fare—with the concession of fish for the male members of the family. The table had been cleaned, and the dishes rinsed for the washer.

"Let's work the table, Tia," Christopher prevailed upon his sister. "I think we all have a lot of questions to ask. Like where we should move, for one."

We had made a preliminary decision to move from Schenectady, New York, but our eventual destination was uncertain.

I had never before consulted a table for assistance in answering my questions.

So much of psychic phenomena, especially that of the seance room, appears to center around a tilting, rapping, or floating table. Certainly in the tradition of my own Scandinavian forebears I was aware that they had used the "table dance" for amusement and for eerie edification on dark, winter nights.

Basically, as I understood it, one posed certain questions which might be answered by knocks or leg-raps for yes or no. I had always thought it apparent that the answers would have to depend at least in some part upon the skillfulness of the inquirers to interpret the explosive responses of the table.

Ever since I was a child I had been told of strange powers

that, under the right conditions, could make the table behave like a ghost and glide across the floor. On occasion, such magnetized tables were said to be able to stand on end and thud the floor so violently that the legs would eventually break off. When such energy was present, I had been advised, the table dance might set other phenomena in motion.

Grandma Anna had told me of seeing pictures fly from their hooks, vases crash to the floor, eerie faces appear at the window panes. She had even said that one could sometimes feel the sensation of unfamiliar fingers about one's face, neck, and shoulders. Puffs of wind could chill the room, and unknown noises and lights could manifest themselves.

In spite of such titillating talk on dark, rainy nights, Grandma Anna only told, she never showed; so I had yet to witness a demonstration of the ancient custom of table tapping. Somehow, as I looked at the guileless faces of Francie's children, I found it very unlikely that I was to witness any genuine phenomena that night. Steve, eager for a new experience, dragged me toward a chair.

I am afraid that I was rather smug as I joined the five children around a somewhat battered card table with a peculiar emblem painted onto its top surface.

"And what is that mystical design?" I asked, deciding to indulge them all the way.

"That's the aegis of Kihief," Tia informed me, tracing the symbol with her forefinger. "Kihief gave that to Mommy to protect us."

Each of the children then reached toward their necks and brought forth chains from beneath shirt or blouse that bore the same emblem engraved on gold medallions.

"See?" Regina asked, as if I needed substantiation of Tia's statement.

The design was that of a shield which bore a crest of a pyramid emblazoned with three lightning, or energy, bolts. At the top of the pyramid was a great eye, suggestive of the Egyptian Eye of Horus.

"Interesting," I pronounced, as Michael and Regina, on either side of me, each clasped one of my hands and bowed their heads. In unison, they began to pray the Lord's Prayer. Once completed, that prayer was followed by a Hail, Mary; several repetitions of Hare Krishna; King David's Twenty-third Psalm, and something that sounded like a verse from either

Kahlil Gibran or the Upanishads.

Francie had certainly taught her kids to be ecumenical, I thought to myself, as Christopher told me that we should now place our palms flat on the table in the manner that Tia had done from the start. The prayers should energize us, I was told.

To my astonishment, a corner of the table elevated itself about nine inches from the floor.

"In the name of the Light, are you a good spirit?" Tia wasted no time in demanding an identification check. "One rap for yes, two for no."

To my relief, the leg tapped once.

"What is your name?" Tia continued with her interrogation.

"A...B...C...D...E..." the children began reciting the letters of the alphabet as the table leg rapped out the name of the visiting spirit by stopping and starting on various letters.

"Aleah," Michael pronounced after the series of rappings had ceased.

Francie had come to stand behind us.

"You must not consider that a name in the sense that we use names," she advised me. "Kihief has said that in their world they exist primarily as vibrational energy patterns. Therefore, it is your repetition of that sound, that vibration, that will put you in touch with that higher energy and in contact with one there who cares very much for your spiritual advancement."

"Aleah," I repeated. "Aleah. A-Lee-ah. I'll remember it, all right. One needs all the help he can get. That must be the name of the female entity that I have seen ever since I was a child."

Tia quizzed Aleah as to my special color (B...L...U...E), my special number (four), my special day (F...R...I...D...A...Y), and my special month (O...C...T...O...B...E...R).

At one point, while the leg was regularly pounding out an answer, I could no longer resist an impulse to test the energy for myself. Somehow, I reasoned, Tia was unconsciously employing a rhythm and a leverage that was raising and lowering the table.

Although my hands were innocently resting flat on the surface of the table in the position that I had been asked to assume, I surreptitiously pressed downward on the dropping thrust of the leg. There would be no question, I thought, that my added weight would hold the table down.

The leg continued its rapping movements unaffected by my deceit.

Intrigued, I exerted as much of my strength as I could without making my treachery an obvious one. There would be no way that the fingertips of a 110-pound teenage girl could counterbalance my 185 pounds.

The leg maintained its measured tapping, and Tia's forearms displayed not the lightest symptom of additional tension or strain.

Somehow, I was forced to admit, there was a force, an energy, animating the table. Somehow, perhaps in a manner similar to the way in which psychic-sensitives channeled energy through the Hieronymous Machine, Tia was focusing the X-Force through the card table beneath her tiny palms.

The evening was filled with a great deal of interesting information, steadily rapped out for us by the energy flowing through Tia to the table.

Steve learned the name of his guardian angel, his color, his day, and so forth. It was revealed that Christopher and I had been brothers in a past life in Greece. Steve, who had just endured an incredible ordeal with me during a motor trip over large expanses of an America gripped by freezing temperatures that dipped below minus-sixty degrees Fahrenheit, was said to have been a brother knight who had once journeyed with me on a great quest.

Then the table leg suddenly crashed to the floor with a much more forceful rap. Once it had our undivided attention, it repeated the violent knocking twice more.

"Mommy," Regina called, "Kihief is in the table."

She made the annoucement as casually as a child in a more conventional household might call her mother to the telephone.

Michael and Regina widened the circle to permit their mother to slide her chair beneath the table. Francie closed her eyes and placed her palms on the aegis of Kihief.

"S...E...D...O...N...A," rapped the table.

"What is a Sedona?" Francie wanted to know.

"M...O...V...E...T...O."

"*Move to Sedona*?" Francie guessed at the message. "We are to move to Sedona?"

The table crashed down on the tapping leg with great emphasis.

"But where is it?" Michael asked.

I explained that Sedona was in Arizona, one of the most beautiful areas in the world. I added that the region had been highly revered by numerous Indian tribes as a sacred place.

Francie shrugged and smiled. "Then that's where we are to move."

Although Francie had never been to Arizona, the word of her guide was all that she needed to know that we were to move to the Southwest. None of the children needed to be persuaded by their mother to accept the verdict. We were moving to Sedona, Arizona.

Shortly before we loaded up the vehicles and the vans, however, Kihief amended his counsel to read that we should rather settle for a time in Paradise Valley. I had been familiar with Sedona, but Paradise Valley drew a blank. It was not until we arrived in Scottsdale and bought our home that we learned the house was in the Paradise Valley area of the Phoenix megalopolis.

We were not the only metaphysical family to have received the message to move to Arizona. When we began to become acquainted in the state, we learned that a remarkable number of psychic sensitives, astrologers, past-life researchers, UFO investigators and the like had recently made their immigration to the area.

"It's almost as if some of us have been conditioned or programmed to come here," Francie has often commented since our arrival in September of 1977. "I feel strongly that Arizona will soon become a mecca for people from all over the United States—perhaps the world—who believe in unity, love, and the spiritual enrichment of themselves and others."

Blossom Ivener observed that people who are "very aware" are "moving to Arizona and finding a path." It is her opinion that more and more individuals who move here will "discover where they're going and realize their destiny."

John Gilliam of the Arizona Society of Astrologers pointed out that the zodiacal chart for Phoenix shows a "high reception factor for newcomers."

Gilliam also said that there is harmony here for the individual: "The atmosphere here is conducive for people to become more open, individualistic, and independent. In Arizona, the vibratory influences make it easier for men and women to get in touch with the psychic side of themselves."

Many of the psychic sensitives with whom I discussed the

matter of their move to Arizona mentioned that they had experienced a strong, almost magnetic, pull to the state. They also remembered a strange period of testing which they had to endure once they arrived here. It was suggested a number of times in our discussions that the desert had always been a place of revelation and ordeal for prophets and mystics.

Viki Johnson agreed: "It's kind of like you have to earn the right to stay here. A lot of people are drawn here, but once they arrive, they find that they hate it. In a sense, they fail the test."

Although the period of testing may have to be endured by many of the New Age people who move to Arizona, Rev. Roger Hight detects an electromagnetic vitality here that sensitizes the body's aura.

"People find that they have more bodily health here," Hight said. "They have a greater ability to accomplish things. It is as if they have a veil lifted from their eyes."

Hight foresees Phoenix gaining in recognition as a great energy center. "People will come here to be rejuvenated. It is as if the surrounding mountains serve as pyramids to focus energy down to us in order to raise our consciousness."

"I feel such a strong Egyptian influence here," Francie has said, and she has painted a number of Egyptian murals on the walls of our home.

"It is possible," she speculates, "that those of us whose Souls once had prior existences in the land of the Nile have been reborn at this time and have been drawn to the Phoenix area."

Viki Johnson has also observed that the influence of Egypt has strongly charged Phoenix. "There are many old souls and Karmic groups reassembling here," she said.

Viki, too, has done her home in an Egyptian theme. "The vibrations of ancient Atlantis are also very much in evidence here," she added.

Rev. John Rodgers of the Alpha Book Center referred me to a small book that had been published by the Order of Omega. Entitled *Phoenix—Spiritual Center,* the volume states that the desert climate attracts psychic sensitives to the city; that ancient civilizations in the area still exert cosmic influences; that Phoenix is one of the Earth's "chakras"; and that Arizona is a place of initiation and testing.

Elsewhere in Arizona, many metaphysicians maintain that

there is a spiritual city which exists above Sedona. This city focuses energy down on the area.

The late Helen Frye told me that Sri Darwin Gross, who was then the spiritual leader of Eckankar, had declared that the waters which run through Oak Creek Canyon have even greater healing properties than the Ganges River of India.

"It is a place of miracles," Ms. Frye said. "Even the animals sense it. My Hopi grandfather told me of seeing the lights of guardian spirits in the area. In Eckankar, we are in attunement with the 'blue light' of our masters and teachers. These lights have also been seen near the spiritual city."

A highly respected scientific specialist, whom we must call "Dr. Elizabeth Keefe" in order to honor her request for anonymity, shared the following remarkable account with us.

One night as she sat late in her office, pondering the significance of her accumulation of statistics, she seemed to feel a strong presence within her. For some reason she could not rationalize, she felt as though she were being directed to hold a pen over a blank sheet of paper.

To her bewilderment—and slight apprehension—her hand began to move wildly across the surface of the paper, looping large circles, scrawling spirals. In the next moment, the moving pen began to form words.

The "presence" who claimed responsibility for the communication identified itself as an etherealized entity who had originally come to Earth from a distant planet thousands of years before. The entity wrote that he and his kind felt a strong kinship with humankind, not only because they were somehow a related species, but because they had implanted their spiritual seed within certain of the more intelligent and physically capable in an organized program of multilevel awareness acceleration for *Homo sapiens*.

The first message had been brief. The entity said that he would like to continue the contact with her. He told her that she was to be a helper of humankind during the coming time of Earth-plane transition.

Elizabeth Keefe had sat back in astonishment when the pen in her hand once again became a regular, immobile writing instrument. How could such a thing have happened to her?

She was a Phi Beta Kappa, who had graduated magna cum laude. Her religious background consisted of having attended a grandfather's funeral in a Roman Catholic church when she was eight. Once, in a survey course of the world's religions, she had read an assigned section of the Bible, along with the Koran, the Upanishads, and the Bhagavad Gita, and other works of inspired writing. She had been somewhat open to psychic sensitivity, regarding it as an atavistic evolutionary function that lingered in some people—as the vestigial appendix and the little toe remained in the greater mass of humankind.

She found herself looking out her office window at the night sky. The entire hypothesis presented by the message was mind-boggling:

A related species had visited Earth from a distant star, implanted their awareness within humankind, before they, themselves, became "etherealized" to a higher dimension of experience. And now, in present time, this genetically transmitted awareness was bursting forth in the consciousness of certain men and women. Once the genetic mechanism had activated these people, they felt strongly imbued with a sense of mission to assist the entire Earthborn species to survive a time of great transformation.

Elizabeth Keefe was puzzled by her experience. When a hard-nosed scientist, such as the one she had always prided herself as being, began to manifest the mental symptoms and expressions of men and women kept under scrutiny by an intolerant society, it was time for rest and relaxation.

The Mountain Shadows resort in Scottsdale, Arizona, was lovely, but her first night there, Elizabeth found herself directed to find a pen and paper. Soon she was writing another message from the entity on Mountain Shadows stationery.

The intelligence communicated that things as humankind presently knew them on Earth were soon to begin to change rapidly. He wrote that it would be a good idea for her to store dry foods and to find a "safe" place in which to live. He told her that she would soon move her practice from Los Angeles to Arizona. Her husband would not accept the changes which were occurring to her.

The entity told of the love that his kind had for humans. It saddened them to know that they could do nothing to avert the cataclysms, the earthquakes, and the disasters that were about to shatter the planet. They could only act as guides to direct humankind to safe places geographically and to responsible courses of action spiritually.

"We are related to you by the creative act of the Father-Mother-Creator Spirit," he told her. "We are on the evolutionary trek together."

The next day, Elizabeth Keefe rented a car and drove north to Sedona. She had a Flair pen and a legal pad at the ready, for that day she was anticipating another communication. The intelligence did not manifest itself through the pen until she stopped for gasoline at an Exxon station in Sedona.

"There is a vortex of energy here that you should experience," the words came, as casually as if directed by a tour guide. Elizabeth's hand transcribed the directions. South at the intersection of 179 and 89A. East at the Airport Road. Continue this road. . . .

And soon she was there, walking up a rather steep incline, being cautious of rattlesnakes on that warm September afternoon, pulling herself past scrub pine, stumbling over an occasional loose rock, avoiding as nimbly as possible the deer droppings scattered near the berry bushes. Then she was descending toward the edge of a steep cliff with a smooth rock shelf. Circling crows overhead seemed to be cawing a warning that a creature without wings must be very surefooted in such terrain.

Elizabeth felt a peculiar tingling in her cheeks. She walked carefully, but eagerly, a bit closer to the cliff's edge. It was breathtakingly lovely here. She could see for miles—thousands of acres of green trees, majestic red rock buttes and mesas, and brilliantly blue sky. She lifted her arms over her head and felt prickles of energy in the palms of her hands. She had found the vortex.

Elizabeth had thrilled to the experience for only a few moments before she was aware of the impulse to write. She moved back to a rock wall and leaned against it as she sat down and propped the legal pad on her knees.

What flowed from the ordinary black Flair pen in her hand was a beautiful salutation to the Christ spirit and the energy that would come to humankind after the cataclysms and the Time of Cleansing had been completed.

The entity explained that "Christ consciousness" referred to a high state of awareness, rather than a single individual.

The Christ energy was one of pure, unconditional love that permitted one to channel in perfect balance a remarkable creative force that existed on Earth, a force that permeated every living thing, a force that was malleable to the human psyche. Those men and women who had achieved the high state of awareness requisite to be "Christed" would be able to manipulate this force in such a positive manner as to fashion literal physical miracles.

When Elizabeth felt the energy of the entity release her hand, she found herself uttering a whispered "Amen."

She became aware that it was nearing sunset. The clerk who had rented her the Chevrolet had told her about the incomparable beauty of the Sedona red rock country at sunset. The man had not simply been speaking in hyperbole for the tourist. Elizabeth had truly never observed a more magnificent setting of the sun.

She rose to her feet, and as she did so, she became aware that something was very different. The entity clearly had not yet left her, but had somehow blended with her. She felt very much as if her own consciousness had been moved off to the sidelines, up in a corner of her brain, and that the essence of the communicating intelligence was occupying the majority of her mind and body.

Elizabeth suddenly began singing out, very loudly, very clearly, but in a language that she did not know—but which sounded to her something like Latin. Somehow she understood that the song issued forth in her own voice had to do with adoration of the creation.

She felt totally integrated with all of life. She was at one with the molecules that comprised the stone beneath her feet. She *was* the crow swooping curiously overhead. She *was* the ground squirrel that peeped out from a clump of grass near a scrub pine. She *was* the scrub pine. She *was* the grass.

Her hands and her arms, then her body, her legs, her feet began to move in a dance. As her body flowed into the dance, her voice released a beautiful song of adoration and joy.

The wind that had been whispering around her ever since she had stepped out on the ledge was now not blowing *on* her, but *through* her; and the entity's hymn expressed a complete integration with all of life's expressions.

Elizabeth had never known such a spirit of joy and celebration. For an incredible moment, she saw her body as the entity perceived it—as an amalgamation of spinning atoms. She knew that, for an indeterminate period of time, she was not a dense body at all.

The four reasons most often mentioned by members of the metaphysical community for their having moved to Arizona might be structured in the following ways:

(1) The desert sand and climate of southern Arizona are conducive to mysticism and psychism.

(2) The powerful energies remaining from the ancient Amerindian and pre-Amerindian civilizations continue to exert a great influence on contemporary psychic sensitives.

(3) Phoenix is destined to become one of the great psychic centers of Earth, and the city has already taken on an "Egyptian" vibration and influence.

(4) Large portions of the state of Arizona will provide "safe" places during the fast-approaching period of cataclysms and Earth changes which so many of the psychics are predicting.

Since 1962 the entire world has been caught up in a kind of psychological upheaval—a deep, far-reaching revolution in the elevation of human consciousness. Whatever their individual paths to the Source, the great majority of the metaphysical community moving to Arizona believe that in order to promote inner peace and world understanding it is necessary to know how mankind has been placed in the whole universal order.

"Once we find a conscious connection with the cosmos, every facet of human existence can be enriched," Francie told me. "The cosmic-spiritual impulse will dispel fear and insecurity in our personal lives and enable us to face our destiny with equanimity. Many of us are convinced that we will be able to see that connection clearer in the deserts and mountains of Arizona."

# Chapter Twelve

## STAR CONSCIOUSNESS

No longer will man be able to see himself entirely unrelated
to mankind, neither will he be able to see mankind unrelated
to life, nor life unrelated to the Universe.

*Teilhard de Chardin*

We will probably learn that Darwin was wrong and that
man came to Earth from another planet . . .

*Buckminster Fuller*

In the 1950s Einstein advised us that humankind had to develop
a new way of thinking if we were to survive as a species. Since
that time, the great genius physicist has not been alone in
suggesting that humankind must develop an inner road to sal-
vation involving a synthesis of rational understanding with the
mystical experience of unity.

As Dr. Sisirkumar Ghose assures us, there need be no quar-
rel between science and spirituality. There are many rooms in
the House of Self, and there are many games to play in the
Garden of God of which Darwin, Marx, or Freud knew nothing.

In 1976, Dr. William Tiller, Department of Materials Science and Engineering, Stanford University, told an audience
of scientists and laymen assembled in Boston for a meeting on

the "new physics of consciousness" that most of the universe
is composed of various, still-hidden, psychoenergies, functioning at different levels in different dimensions. At our five-
sense level, Dr. Tiller explained, we are incapable of perceiving
ultimate reality, but somewhere, which we feebly identify as
the "Source," all levels are one, and Time-Space-Matter are
all mutable.

The physicist also asserted that our species appears to be
undergoing a biological transformation at the present time that
is occuring so widely in the human family as to appear to be
mutational.

The many paths that I have trod on my quest have demonstrated to my satisfaction that true magic still lives. And I
am convinced that if we but permit it to be so, the years lying
before us can be the most magical and mystical in all of history—for we are approaching an opportunity of transformation
for our entire species.

When I consider the implications of the awakening seed
within our species, I am reminded that to be human is to be
different from a bird, a dog, a flower. Once we as humans
have reached our biological attainment, we respond to the spiritual seed within us that dictates that we begin to work on
ourselves in some way to develop our own consciousness so
that we might bring about the next stage of evolution. It is as
if we have first to be conscious of a possible destiny before
that destiny may be achieved.

I perceive that Francie's concept of "Star Consciousness"
will be the prime requisite of humankind's next stage of evolution. Such consciousness requires that one develops an awareness of his or her potential abilities as a sovereign entity and
yet retains the perspective of one who views the planet from
the stars and understands that all life is One upon its surface.
Such an attitude encourages a sense of responsibility and a
feeling of unconditional love toward all living things.

It is as Reza Arasteh, a transcultural developmental psychologist, author of *Final Integration in the Adult Personality*,
has remarked—humankind must physically separate itself from
Earth so that it can feel the Universe: "The Cosmic Self is the
manifestation of transcending the earthly and cultural self."

Writing in *Fields Within Fields . . . Within Fields*, Volume
4, Number 1, 1971, Arasteh said:

... All major cultures have transcended cultural reality through certain mechanisms known as Judaic, Christian, or Moslem mysticism in the Near East; humanism and modern psychoanalysis in the West; and Zen Buddhism and Taoism in Far Eastern cultures. The interesting point is that all these mechanisms have come to us as a "path" rather than as logic, as experience rather than rationality. Regardless of language or cultural and temporal differences, all these styles of life have adopted the same goal of experiencing man in his totality, and the reality of all is cosmic reality... The common denominator, the process of breakthrough, comes with encounter and inner motivation, and the result is inner freedom for a cosmic trip and outer security for the release of unbound energy for future creativity....

In the years of transition which lie ahead, I shall rely upon the inner promptings which I receive from Aleah and upon the channelings of my own personal mystic, Francie.

You need not marry a mystic to receive his or her guidance, but I strongly suggest that you pay increasing heed to the messages which the mystics are beginning to share on an accelerated program for the elevation of mass awareness.

In his *Mystics as a Force for Change*, Dr. Sisirkumar Ghose states wisely that, instead of accusing the mystics of being dropouts and escapists, "it might be fairer to say that in breaking the illusions of the cave dwellers they have been more responsible to reality and to the race. In the alchemy of awareness, they have been the true scientists of catharsis and conversion, the piercing of the planes, which is another name for the ascent of man. The only radical thinkers, they alone go to the root of the matter, beyond the various shaky schemes of mundane perfection, swaying between the worship of the Fatted Calf and the horror of the Organization Man."

I think it may well be argued that, throughout the evolution of humankind, the mystics have always been among us as evidence of transitional forms within our species. The mystics have always been those who have most strongly sensed the growth of the spiritual seed within our psyches.

As Dr. Ghose says it:

The mystic's real task for service to the race is not so
much to help men solve problems in their all-too-human
ways, as to transcend secular and humanistic values, to
transfigure them in the light of the spiritual ideal or the
will of God. The mystic brings not peace, but the sword
of discrimination and a sense of the holy, a sacramental
attitude in all the ways of one's being. . . .

The mystics have played an important, and enormous,
part in the making of man and civilization. Most early
civilizations owe a good deal to this creative minority.
In the absence of a sharp division of labor, such as has
marked the later periods of our history, the early mystics
would also be among the priests and medicine-men of
the tribe. (The role is neither extinct nor anachronis-
tic). . . .

Sri Aurobindo writes in the *Life Divine* that however the
person of spiritual realization lives, acts, and behaves, he or
she lives always in the Divine.

"In our present life of Nature," he remarks, "in our externalized surface existence, it is the world that seems to create
us; but in the turn to the spiritual life it is we who must create
ourselves and our world. In this new formula of creation, the
inner life becomes the first importance, and the rest can be
only its expression and outcome. It is this, indeed, that is
indicated by our own strivings toward perfection, the perfection
of our own soul and mind and life and the perfection of the
life of the race."

In the New Age which lies ahead, men and women with
awareness must begin to understand the world in terms of new
principles, new visions of reality, and new boundaries of human
potential. Prejudices must be exposed as chaotic and destruc-
tive. Rituals and traditions must be evaluated as to whether or
not they support or distract the individual while he or she is
making an effective transition into the future.

Happiness in the New Age that is dawning for humankind
cannot be accomplished merely by doing new things in new
ways. Deserting the concrete canyons of the city for the soft
grasses of the forest, dropping flesh foods for a vegetarian diet,
ceasing concentration for meditation, will not of themselves
bring immediate contentment. Those who will be happiest and
most productive in the years which lie ahead will be those men

and women who understand that they live in a participatory universe and that it is by their actions and their beingness that they will reveal their divine origins.

Certain men and women who claim prophetic inspirations have emphasized the promise of our metamorphosis into Cosmic Humankind. Other visionaries have told us that humankind is moving into a new activating archetype, the Cosmic Person—humankind in symbiotic relationship to the universe at large.

No longer can we permit ourselves to be victims of a vengeful God or a hostile Nature. The world which we will behold will be the world which we have cocreated with Higher Intelligence.

From what I can understand and envision, our future on this planet is likely to encompass a total mutation in our biological structure, as well as our consciousness and our social norms.

Secular authorities in the physical sciences, from Einstein to Buckminster Fuller, have been warning us, for decades now, that we will have to alter our psyches or the magnification of our foul tempers through technology will destroy our material world.

The time is long overdue to permit the daring new sciences to have their day.

Let us see if radionics can blend the superconscious mind together with physical instrumentation in order to diagnose and treat diseases in humans, animals, and plants.

Let us witness the psychotronic generators combining human and machine so that the psyche and its sensory apparatus may serve as amplifier, resonator, antenna, or psychological transfer mechanism.

Let us test the claims that such "living machines" can permit an interaction at a distance between, and among, people and the surrounding world—both animate and inanimate.

If we remain open to the exploration of the possibility of an as yet unidentified force in nature, an "X-Force," then we may be able to explain all psychic abilities. We may, therefore, come to perceive "bioplasma" as a "fifth state of matter," and we will understand why the field of biopsychophysics regards a human being as an astoundingly complex electrical entity.

And if we but permit more extensive experimentation, we may learn that the "auras" that psychic sensitives have long claimed to "read" may prove to be the life-field of electromagnetic energy that surrounds all living things.

As we stretch our imaginations into the future, we are certain to be challenged by unconventional archaeologists and anthropologists who insist that we must truly understand our yesterdays before we run haphazardly into tomorrow. Already there are digs being conducted which will produce remarkable artifacts indicative of an astonishing prehistory for humankind.

And, quite likely, the more we explore our past in order to open doors to the future, we will discover that we are also opening the gates to the true Kingdom of God.

Elaine Pagels, writing in *The Gnostic Gospels*, presents us with a translation of the *Gospel of Thomas*, which tells us that, far from legitimizing any earthly institution, Jesus directed those who would listen to their own inner capacity to find their own direction to the "light within": "There is a light within a man of light, and it lights up the whole world. If he does not shine, he is darkness."

What is more, according to the *Gospel of Thomas*, Jesus ridiculed those who thought of the Kingdom of God in literal terms, as if it were a specific place. The synoptic gospels, as passed down to us through innumerable councils and decrees and translations, have as one of Jesus' principal teachings the coming of the Kingdom of God as an actual event to be expected in history. In the *Gospel of Thomas*, Pagels' translation, Jesus says otherwise:

> . . . the Kingdom is inside of you, and it is outside of you. When you come to know yourselves, then . . . you will realize that you are the sons of the living Father. But if you will not know yourselves, then you dwell in poverty, and it is you who are that poverty.

> When will the New World come?

> He said to them, "What you look forward to has already come, but you do not recognize it."

It would seem likely that to Jesus the Kingdom of God actually represented a state of transformed consciousness:

> "Shall we, then, as children enter the Kingdom?" Jesus said to them. "When you make the two one, and when you make the inside like the outside and the outside like

the inside, and the above like the below, and when you
make the male and the female one the same . . . you will
enter the [Kingdom]."

In August of 1981, three American scholars found a cere-
monial imitation of the Ark of the Covenant in Palestine.

As this is being written, there are at least sixty sites currently
under excavation in the Holy Land. King Solomon's mines and
the ruins of Sodom and Gomorrah have already been discovered. And so have eight previously missing pages of the *Codex
Sinaiticus*, a Greek version of the Old Testament.

Experts are now translating manuscripts which cover the
two-hundred-year gap between the Old and New Testaments.
These texts were originally left out of the Bible because the
religious councils that put the versions of scripture together
decided that the scripts taught angel worship.

I suspect that today, once the manuscripts are translated,
we shall perceive them as instructions on how best to establish
communication with those Light Beings who care about our
spiritual evolution. These texts may even tell us more about
the Star Beings who shepherded specially selected early humans
to blend their genes to create "giants in the Earth."

There are certain sincere visionaries who are convinced that
our planet shall experience a global UFO encounter in the year
1999, and a number of recent motion pictures would seem to
be the result of an active campaign of positive programming
to insure a hospitable reception for such an extraterrestrial visitation. We have survived the "wars of the worlds" which
panicked us in the early dramas presented by radio, television,
and motion pictures; we have endured the bug-eyed monsters
that came to enslave us; we have outlasted the hideous creatures
that sought to eat both ourselves and our cities. It would appear
that our collective unconscious is at last ready for a friendly
encounter with other citizens of the Cosmos.

Stanley Kubrick's and Arthur C. Clarke's *2001: A Space
Odyssey* told us of an ancient alien artifact that had stimulated
the brain of prehuman ape creatures so that evolution would
one day propel humankind back to its place of origin.

Gene Rodenberry's television series *Star Trek* portrayed a
partnership between humankind and aliens (epitomized by the
friendship of Kirk and Spock) which was sustained by mutual
respect. Rodenberry's scripts seemed to indicate that such unions

could permit humankind to go boldly to new frontiers beyond the stars.

The *Star Wars* series of motion pictures focus upon conflicts between intergalactic cultures which occurred aeons before our world had come into being. At the same time that we are viewing a transplantation of human emotions and dreams, Yoda, a pointy-eared, reptilian humanoid, is teaching us about the existence of a Force that interpenetrates all of matter and which may be controlled by the psyche of a disciplined practitioner.

*Close Encounters of the Third Kind* was Steven Spielberg's way of making sense of random UFO sightings and contacts. Spielberg's greatest gift to theater audiences lay in his permitting us to have a spiritual experience when the dazzling mother ship landed and bombarded us with eerie, archetypal shocks of recognition. Now, in the summer of 1982, he is introducing us to an amphibian-reptilian entity who literally lives on the love vibration and who is apparently a member of an extraterrestrial species who has been monitoring our plants, our soils, and ourselves for God knows how long.

Francie's guide, Kihief, told her several years ago that she would live through the killer carrots, the hungry blobs, and the rampaging robots to be able to view the kind of motion pictures that would be designed to prepare all of humankind for a positive encounter with an extraterrestrial species.

"There is a basic longing in each of us for our true home, our parent civilization beyond the stars," Francie has often remarked. "Such films as those which are currently being released have been inspired by Higher Intelligences so that our feelings of being so homesick would be eased. At the same time, we are being promised that our odyssey will one day be completed."

Dr. William A. Tiller thinks that humankind has "turned the corner" back toward an inner knowledge of the Oneness of its species and is "heading home again."

In his "Three Relationships of Man" (*Proceedings of the A. R. E. Medical Symposium*, Phoenix, Arizona, January 1975), Dr. Tiller postulates the following:

We have come from advanced societies whose special technologies suited the great mental capacities of the inhabitants, and we are heading back in the same direction. We have come from societies where the inhabitants reliably sensed deeper dimensions of the universe . . . and they manipulated space, time, and matter with their minds. We are heading back in the same direction. . . .

In addressing the problems of man in relationship to his "local self," Dr. Tiller stresses that we must learn that that which appears to us on the "outer" is but a materialized reflection of what is on the "inner."

> What we dislike in our society cannot be effectively changed from the outside because it is only symptomatic of that which is inside us. The only real change takes place within us. We must change *there* and then the outer consistent materialization will naturally occur . . . *We* are the *product* of the process and *we* are transformed by the process. . . .
>
> . . . We must also learn that we are *One* at the level of self that pushes the switches in our simulators—and that we are here for a good and valid reason. Evolution for all is ultimately necessary for evolution of the one. It is a family task and ultimately can only be solved as a family. And, as all families know, the only effective working fluid is love. . . .
>
> We may wish for the masses of humanity to show more altruistic and more highly motivated ideals than they presently do. *However, it will become enlightened only if we believe it is possible for it to do so and if we act as if it were already well on the path to doing so!*

Dr. Tiller reminds us that all of the things that we do in life are individual acts of creation. If we are to be effective creators, he suggests four important steps that we might consider with each meaningful act:

1. We must clearly *visualize* our intention;
2. We must build a strong *desire* to achieve that intention;
3. We must develop the *faith* that the visualization can be achieved; and
4. We must exercise the *will* to make it manifest, i.e., work at it.

Struggle, Dr. Tiller advises us, is to be anticipated on the Earth plane: *"If the medium in which we wish to create offers us no resistance, then we can make no durable impression. We must expect to struggle!"*

Call it a dream, a vision, a fantasy, whatever you wish. Fit the following experience into your reality however you must.

On an evening in October of 1981, I was sitting quietly in my office, deeply immersed in contemplation. I had begun my time in the Silence by observing that October has always been a special month for me. I have also felt that it is a special time for the "Other." I feel that it is no coincidence that, for so many men and women throughout the centuries, October has been a month of mystery, as well as harvest.

I believe that there are reasons beyond our understanding that make it easier for the other world, the higher dimension, to make contact with us during the month of October. I think that this may be due to some cyclic manifestation of time of which we as yet have no true knowledge.

After I had contemplated this matter for a few minutes, I felt a beautiful sense of Oneness moving over me as my level of consciousness slipped deeper into the Silence. I visualized a golden circle of protection; and, as I did so, it seemed to me as though I could actually see a palpable, pulsating, ring of golden light moving around me.

Lovely multicolored ripples of energy began to swirl around me, and I closed my eyes.

When next I opened them, it seemed to me as though I were now seated in the midst of a colorful garden.

It was a lovely summer's day—somewhere—and the garden seemed almost to glow with flowers of every conceivable hue. Birds called to one another from a nearby grove of trees. Insects buzzed and clacked from grasses tufted near a musically trickling stream. The air was as fresh and as sweet as spring honey.

I recognized the garden as the place where, in my dreams and meditations, I had encountered Aleah. And whether the City of God is without or within, whether I had traveled through outer space or inner space, I was now in the presence of this lovely embodiment of the feminine creative principle.

As always in my dreams and inspirations, Aleah wore a white robe trimmed in gold, suggestive, to my appraisal, of a

Grecian or a Roman style. On her chest there hung suspended a large crystal set in gold. It seemed to me that I could hear her welcome to me spoken in a warm contralto voice.

I was told that I was seeing the place which Aleah and her kind had fashioned for themselves in a frequency above the Earth's vibrations. Here, she said, they evolved still higher, continuing their ascent to the eventual goal of all creation, that of becoming One with the Source of All That Is.

*Was this what might be called the fourth dimension?*

It would be better, I was informed, if I thought of the place as an "in-between universe," for they had impressed their thought and memory patterns upon the frequency of the stellar environment and had fashioned a facsimile of their home. She bade me to follow her to the top of a grassy hill to see before us their thought-memory recreation of Leahlan, one of their favorite cities on their world.

Stretching before us, clearly visible from the top of the hill, was a beautiful city of white buildings with tall spires, towers, and turrets. Occasionally, there appeared to be a structure made of crystal, with each of its facets reflecting the Sun. There were also a number of golden buildings, which I assume were temples. Leahlan was apparently a harbor, for a remarkably blue sea touched an expanse of white beach just before some of the farther buildings.

I remembered the time that Francie and I had once perceived a vivid projection of the city on the wall of a room while we were meditating. We had both somehow recognized the place as Leahlan.

Aleah laughed softly and told me that Francie and I had seen the city in memories which they had been projecting toward us since childhood.

*Then was it as Francie had said? Was this our true home beyond the stars?*

Aleah said that it would seem so because we were their spiritual inheritors.

*Where had their world really been?*

Their physical world died in a brilliant blaze of glory that our science calls a supernova. Their home existed now only in their memory-thought patterns, as they externalized them here— and as they had seeded them within us.

Neither did Aleah exist as I perceived her. She had only assumed her former physical pattern so that she might better communicate with me. She was now a being of light energy, who assumed such a form only when it pleased her to remember something or when it became necessary to interact according to a structured pattern.

She nodded back toward the garden, causing her long yellow hair to sway slightly, as if a gentle breeze had caught it. The shimmering bluish white flashes of light around the flowers were others of her kind who had come to see me.

I thought of how Kihief had materialized before Francie when she was a child. He had seemed as solid as she. I recalled other multidimensional beings, including Aleah, who had materialized before me.

Aleah explained that Earth was a dimension of much lower vibrational frequencies. Earth was a place of form and substance and pattern. Whenever a multidimensional being was forced to manifest on the Earth plane, he or she had to assume form and substance.

They had no choice in the matter, Francie had once channelled. Their energy was forced into a material pattern.

That was why the multidimensional beings could manifest themselves only for brief moments of Earth time. They could not risk becoming locked once again into Earth frequencies. They could, literally, be trapped in our material world. They could be regressed thousands of years in their spiritual-physical evolution.

My feelings of longing for an extensive communication with Aleah and her kind in a material form on Earth was met with her reminder that they were always accessible to us through meditation, dreams, and visions.

Each of the Starseed had a mission to complete, Aleah stressed. Contact with one's inner awareness would guide him or her to fulfill such a mission in earnest.

*Were there those who might seek to block our mission?* The laws of polarity made this so, Aleah conceded, but we were children of light, love, and truth. We must go into the world freely expressing the awareness of who we were. We would be stronger, she said, if we conducted our mission in twos— male and female—balancing our energies.

We must prepare the people of Earth who were ensnared by materialism for the opportunity of transformation that awaited them, Aleah instructed me. We must help them survive the times of dramatic Earth changes and social upheaval that were even now beginning on the planet.

We must aid those who have been seduced by their lower, carnal, selves. We must help them to receive their spiritual initiation, so that all those of the Earthborn species might be transmuted to a higher frequency of energy, a finer vibration of matter.

Within our essential selves, Aleah told me, was that highest aspect of the creative mind, the Christ consciousness. It was that aspect that would enable us to reflect our pure Soul energy and to balance the X-Force so that it would always be used for good. It was the seed of the Christ consciousness that had for so long lain dormant in the psyches of the Earthborn children.

In the next instant, Aleah and her world had disappeared, and I was alone again in my office.

Whether the remarkable experience of that October night had a reality beyond that of a profound vision, I may never know—but of one thing I am certain: It is only a matter of time before each of us on this planet experiences a much larger universe.

For the skeptical who are unwilling to accept the explanations for humankind's remarkable longing for the stars which I have presented in this book, let me attempt one last very physical reason why we might feel homesick whenever we gaze up at the heavens.

A growing number of scientists have been steadily amassing evidence that the Earth may have been seeded with life from outer space by means of meteorites, "shooting stars," that slammed onto this planet in some vast antiquity. These geochemists and astrogeologists have stated that within the fragments of certain meteorites they have detected predominant quantities of the kind of amino acids (the building blocks of proteins) that most commonly occur in living things. Although the concept is controversial, the implication of such research is that the beginnings of life on this planet were seeded by shooting stars.

If those essential sparks of life did indeed come from the cosmos, then we are all, most certainly, "star people"; and we would have good reason to feel nostalgia as we look up at the welcoming vastness of the night sky. And now, as we begin our first feeble attempts at leaving this planet to begin expanding our reach to other worlds, we should understandably know that we are returning home.

In the March 1982 issue of *Omni* magazine, Nobel Prize winner Dr. Francis Crick, the scientist who discovered the DNA molecule, spoke of his provocative theory that our planet had been "seeded" by intelligent life from a distant planet. Astonished by the uniformity of the genetic code on Earth, Dr. Crick conceived the theory of directed panspermia.

When questioned as to the method by which such galactic farmers may have arrived here with their seeds in our prehistory, Dr. Crick responded by saying:

> Either you have a rocket manned with people who can somehow survive all that time through successive generations . . . or you need unmanned rockets carrying some other form of life . . . There are technical problems, but none, I should think, that couldn't be solved by us, for example, within a few hundred years.

> *What form of life would have been sent by those intelligences who seeded our planet?*

> When you look at all of the options, it turns out that perhaps the most attractive one would be to send bacteria. They are small, and can be frozen for long periods of time, and can survive upon arrival under many adverse conditions that would kill more advanced life forms. And, of course, they may have used gene-splicing techniques and the like to create bacterial forms best suited for the prebiotic conditions of the target planets.

Sir Fred Hoyle, internationally recognized British astronomer and mathematician, has directly challenged the Darwinian concept of a gradual terrestrial evolution from some primordial ooze. In *EVOLUTION FROM SPACE* (Simon and Schuster, 1982), Hoyle, in collaboration with Chandra Wickramasinghe, states that life on Earth stemmed from microgenetic fragments from outer space which were "exactly the right size to ride on the light waves of stars."

The two British scientists declare that our planet received

life with the "fundamental biochemical problems already solved." The source of such solutions was an intelligence whose purpose was to spread life "in an elegant way." This "intelligence" may be a series of question marks or God, Hoyle concludes, but "the new evidence points clearly and decisively to a cosmic origin of life on Earth."

Don't shrug off these concepts. There are those scientists who believe that consciousness of some sort exists in each living cell. There are evolutionists who theorize that at a certain stage of our development the individual cells and cell units that collected into our body parts all had consciousness and that they deliberately formed groupings which evolved into a single unit with a unique life function and a collective sense of oneness. In other words, these millions of cells formed specialized organs, glands, muscles, bones, and so forth, which maintained a constant cooperative energy flow. The aggregate of their cooperation became a body, an "all." To a single cell, however, the All may be "God."

If the original cells of life on this planet came from outer space, then the memory of being "star stuff" which evolved to humankind could be as much a part of each sentient being as is the memory of having been a "dragon" in Eden.

But as would be obvious to the most casual reader of this book, I have come to accept a spiritual, as well as a physical, origin of humankind's ever-emerging Star Consciousness.

If you dare to heed the summons of the seed within you and set forth on your own quest in a desire to fulfill your own mission, I can promise you that you will become increasingly aware of your connection to all that was, is, and shall be.

You will discover your different levels of being, your inner abilities, and how to use them in loving service to humankind.

You will gain the exciting knowledge that you can, in concert with Higher Intelligence, create your own reality to achieve everything that is necessary for your transcendence from fragmentation into wholeness. You will learn that you have within you the cosmic awareness which can answer all of life's problems and provide you with the knowledge of how to link up with the external Source of infinite wisdom. The Kingdom of God is first reached within, then connected to the Cosmos.

And as you remain steadfast on your quest, completing your mission, we shall meet one day, you and I, and we shall join hands and begin to mold the future. We shall together fashion a New Age in which the principle of spirituality will be placed before that of materiality. We shall create a world whose citizens will never lose sight of the fact that the essence of humanity is its intellect and its enduring spirit.

True to the seed which grows strong within our psyches, we shall teach the children of tomorrow that the lasting truths are not those of machines, associations, political parties, trade balances, and computers, but those of imagination, inspiration, the soul's evolution, and the Oneness of All That Is.

Peace, Love, Light,
Brad Steiger
Scottsdale, Arizona